My Ascent of Mont Blanc

WITH A PREFACE BY

DERVLA MURPHY

Translated from the French
by Jennifer Barnes

HarperCollins*Publishers,*
77–85 Fulham Palace Road,
Hammersmith, London W6 8JB

Published by HarperCollins*Publishers* 1992
9 8 7 6 5 4 3 2 1

First published in France by Les Éditions Arthaud, Paris, 1987

A catalogue record for this book is
available from the British Library

ISBN 0 00 215717 9

Typeset in Linotron Bembo at
The Spartan Press Ltd,
Lymington, Hampshire

Printed in Great Britain by
HarperCollins Book Manufacturing Glasgow

IN MEMORY OF

ANDREW NEIL CROMPTON,

1964–1985,

WHO DIED CLIMBING

ABOVE CHAMONIX.

CONTENTS

ILLUSTRATIONS

PREFACE

On 4 September 1838, standing 15,782 feet above the sea, Henriette d'Angeville, a fervent royalist, drank the health of the Comte de Paris in lemonade. It was 1.30 pm and her thermometer read eight degrees below zero in the sun. Within seven minutes her pulse rate – regularly checked all the way to the top of Europe's highest mountain – had dropped to 108 beats a minute. Then, somewhat melodramatically, she released a carrier pigeon to convey her good news to Chamonix: for the first time, a lady stood on the summit of Mont Blanc. Chamonix of course already knew; by then the observation of climbing parties was among the village's main tourist attractions.

For some fifty years, Chamonix had been on the Grand Tour trail and its many famous visitors included Goethe, Victor Hugo, Alexandre Dumas, Shelley and Byron. The last remarked to Hobhouse, 'It is like a dream, something too brilliant and wild for reality.' But none of these men, however addicted they might have been to physical exercise, even considered an ascent of Mont Blanc. In the 1830s, mountaineering seemed a masochistic eccentricity, unless it had some serious commercial or scientific purpose. Most people still agreed with John de Bremble, the medieval monk who had prayed, while crossing the Great Saint Bernard, 'Lord, restore me to my brethren, that I may tell them that they come not to this place of torment.' When Whymper was scrambling among the Alps, during the 1860s, he often commented in the same key: 'The teeth chattered involuntarily – talking was laborious; the breath froze instantaneously; eating was disagreeable; sitting was impossible.'

Small wonder, then, that Mlle d'Angeville's resolve to attempt Mont Blanc caused 'a general outcry of amazement and disapproval' among Geneva neighbours 'particularly prone to a general conformity of manners and behaviour'. When asked to explain her unseemly ambition she gave an answer that outshines all other replies, from Mallory onwards, to that tiresome 'Why?':

> 'The soul has needs, as does the body, peculiar to each individual; and a desire to subordinate these needs to the general rule is as unreasonable as an attempt to bring up the weak on precepts laid down for the strong or vice versa . . . In short, each of us must arrange his life according to his moral or intellectual inclinations. And so it is just as ridiculous to ask someone who is fond of travel, "Why are you setting out?" as it is to say, "Why are you staying at home?", to someone who loves seclusion.'

Predictably, this explanation only irritated Mlle d'Angeville's critics and while preparing for her 'excursion' she was forced to instruct a maidservant thus: 'Jeannette, if anyone calls to see me, you will say that I am not at home . . . There are to be no exceptions.'

A backward leap of the imagination is required to appreciate Mlle d'Angeville's courage. In 1838, the ascent of Mont Blanc was truly perilous and everyone still fearfully remembered the first recorded Alpine accident, the deaths of three guides in 1820, as they led an English party up the *ancien passage* above the Rochers Rouges. Moreover, Henriette d'Angeville was challenging not only Europe's highest mountain, but a degree of prejudice that would have defeated most people. Ladies were not supposed to do Things Like That. The 'naturally strong constitution' to which Mlle d'Angeville refers in her Introduction was generally regarded as a peasant quality, not an attribute of which ladies should boast, and certainly not one to be displayed by climbing a mountain most gentlemen preferred to admire from afar.

For obvious reasons, women climbers have always provoked male hostility. When Fanny Workman died in 1925, the *Alpine Journal* pompously conceded:

> 'She herself felt that she had suffered sex-antagonism and it is possible that some unconscious feeling, let us say, of the novelty of a woman's intrusion into the domain of exploration so long reserved to men may in some quarters have existed . . .'

By 1977 it had repeatedly been proved, on Everest and elsewhere, that gender is not what differentiates the mountaineering élite from the rest of us. Yet when Arlene Blum then sought approval for the first (and successful) attempt on Annapurna by an all-woman team, the American Alpine Club was sullenly reluctant to co-operate – 140 years after a woman, unaided by modern equipment and techniques, had climbed Mont Blanc. It is significant that by 1838 Mlle d'Angeville – plainly not an irresolute woman – had been coveting that summit for ten years. Perhaps she needed the self-assurance bestowed by Time – in recompense for what it takes away – to enable her so spectacularly to defy the conventions.

A drawing in the library of Geneva University, by F. Hibert, shows Mlle d'Angeville inspecting her Chamonix guides on the morning of the 3rd of September, 1838. This sketch does not suggest that she was about to scale Mont Blanc; her clothing, weighing twenty-one pounds, seems more of a potential hazard than any number of crevasses, loose rocks or sudden storms. Under a voluminous belted cloak she wore fleece-lined plaid, peg-top trousers and thick woollen stockings over silk stockings. A close fur-trimmed bonnet with a green veil matched a long black boa, a black velvet face-mask and deep fur cuffs. Yet even this bizarre ensemble was more restrained than the clothing of Henry Atkins, who had climbed Mont Blanc a year previously, wearing two of everything and three of most things.

Mlle d'Angeville's special equipment consisted only of a long, awkward-looking alpenstock, unchanged since the first ascent of the mountain in 1786. Mountaineering techniques, in our sense, were as yet unknown. Ropework remained rudimentary and the weighty wooden ladders used for crossing crevasses needed exceptionally strong men to carry them – men who consumed vast quantities of food. The d'Angeville expedition's numerous guides – laden as though for an Everest assault – also had to carry fodder to sustain the riding-mule at the centre of Hibert's sketch, whose assistance was scorned by Mlle d'Angeville. Always an enthusiastic trekker among her beloved Alps, she was as fit as any of her guides at the age of forty-four. With her brother, the Count Adolphe d'Angeville, she had been brought up in Lomprès Castle, on the 3000-foot, sternly magnificent Jurassic plateau, where the dome of Mont Blanc was visible in clear weather and the long winters bred hardy folk.

To modern readers, Mlle d'Angeville's massive support-team and elaborate pre-climb precautions may seem absurd. But we would be mistaken to mock them or to smile at her engagingly unconcealed pride as she returned to Chamonix in triumph. Her ebullient account of this three-day adventure reminds us of the power, both positive and negative, of mind over matter. Nowadays many travellers trek lengthily through the Andes or the Himalayas at 15,000 feet or higher, quite unperturbed – though much slowed – by their bodies' well-understood reactions to thin air. But, when little was known about the effects of high altitudes, these were always disconcerting and could be terrifying. During her descent, Mlle d'Angeville marvelled that she could move with ease, instead of having to stop every few yards to regain breath: 'I was completely free from those disorders which had been such a torment to me only a few hours earlier in exactly the same place.'

Before descending, Mlle d'Angeville took detailed notes and

her description of what she saw and felt is both factual and lyrical. Unlike Edward Whymper, she did not consider the view from the summit 'unsatisfactory'. Whymper grumbled, 'There is nothing to look up to; all is below . . . The man who is there is somewhat in the position of one who has attained all that he desires – he has nothing to aspire to.' Mlle d'Angeville was less illogical and more sensitive. Relishing her achievement, she likened the panorama to 'an immense picture-gallery, laid out as a reward for the danger the intrepid explorer has encountered on the way up.' A woman friend advised that her account of the climb should 'bear the feminine stamp' – and it does.

Henriette d'Angeville was not the first woman to reach the summit of Mont Blanc; in 1809 an eighteen-year-old Chamonix maid-servant, Marie Paradis, had made the ascent. But she hardly counted, having been dragged up the last several stages, in an altitude-induced semi-coma, by her villager companions. As Mlle d'Angeville noted, 'When I went up Mont Blanc it had not been ascended by any woman capable of remembering her impressions.' She herself firmly rejected all offers of help, beyond what was customary for guides to offer gentlemen climbers. It had become essential for her to prove to the world – perhaps especially to the censorious Geneva world – that a lady, unaided, could reach this summit. Later, in a flippant moment, she did herself an injustice by making her much-quoted remark about having climbed Mont Blanc merely to gain as much publicity as George Sand. (The novelist had recently startled Chamonix by appearing in her ideologically significant male garb, accompanied by a youth dressed as a woman.) In fact Henriette d'Angeville was a dedicated mountaineer who made her last and twenty-first climb – the 10,250-foot Oldenhorn – at the age of sixty-nine, eight years before her death. By then the Right Hon. Sir Alfred Wills had climbed the Wetterhorn above Grindelwald – in 1854 – thus establishing himself as the pioneer of mountaineering *as a sport*. However, Mlle d'Angeville, who tackled Mont Blanc some twenty years before the founding of the Alpine Club, deserves to be remembered as one of the bravest pioneers of mountaineering *for fun*.

DERVLA MURPHY

Translator's Note

Henriette d'Angeville's spelling of proper names is sometimes idiosyncratic, especially when they are English. I have taken the liberty of correcting those that could be checked; a valuable source has been *The Annals of Mont Blanc* by C. E. Mathews, London, 1898.

INTRODUCTION

During the months of July and August 1838 I had visited the valleys of Montjoie and Chamonix, had seen and admired some of the delightful views they offer, and had concluded my excursion with a trip to Mont Joli[1] and one to le Jardin[2]. On neither of these walks did I suffer the fatigue commonly experienced by travellers; perhaps this good fortune was due as much to a naturally strong constitution, invigorated by the pure air of the high mountains that are my home,[3] as to the habit I had formed in early youth of crossing the steep slopes and deep valleys of the country of my birth.

Montjoie and Chamonix lie at the very foot of Mont Blanc, and I could not be so close to it without my old longing to climb it returning more powerfully than ever.

There are some people who, once they have come to a decision, must embark straight away on those preparations that will lead to its fulfilment, and I confess that I am one of them. I do not boast of this, for I know that opinions differ, and am only too well aware that some will condemn as haste and imprudence what others will praise as purpose and determination.

On my return to Geneva, I communicated my plan to a few close friends; the news spread like wildfire and immediately occasioned much gossip and speculation.

I know few places in which it is more pleasant to live than Geneva, where friendships, once formed, are more stable, and where malice in social intercourse is less common. I must, however, admit that its inhabitants are particularly prone to a general conformity of manners and behaviour, and are uncommonly surprised by any action that deviates from the ordinary pattern of life. So, when it became known that Mlle d'Angeville, just back from Chamonix, was intending to return in order to attempt an ascent on Mont Blanc, there was a general outcry of amazement and disapproval, invariably introduced by the words, 'But what an extraordinary idea!', followed by, 'She must be prevented from such madness.'

And off they would troop to tug at my doorbell at all hours, first to confirm the truth of this rumour, and then to torment me with a very battery of questions.

'Why this sudden craving for travel?'

'You have just come from Chamonix and yet you want to return?'

'Why?' is indeed an ill-advised little word on the lips of those who are not close friends; I shall, nevertheless, try to give some response here to all those who questioned me about my trip to Mont Blanc.

So, my reply to the first 'why?' is this: The soul has needs, as does the body, peculiar to each individual; and a desire to subordinate these needs to the general rule is as unreasonable as an attempt to bring up the weak on precepts laid down for the strong, or vice versa. Now, some yearn for the sweet peace of country life, others for the tumult of a great city and the intoxicating distractions of society; some aspire to the austerities of monastic life, some are drawn to study, and others seek the change and activity inherent in a life of travel. In short, each of us must arrange his life according to his moral or intellectual inclinations. And so it is just as ridiculous to ask someone who is fond of travel, 'Why are you setting out?', as it is to say, 'Why are you staying at home?', to someone who loves seclusion. The natural response from both would be, 'Because that is where I find my peculiar pleasure and happiness'.

Why not travel where everyone goes? Switzerland or Italy, for example.

Whatever precautions may be taken, every journey brings with it a whole host of small aggravations. In my view, the only compensation for these is the charm of novelty. Now, this is not to be found on a tour of countries already described a hundred times, of which all the most favoured views have been reproduced in faithful sketches, the various national costumes painted and the folk-songs collected. Indeed, to go further, I much fear that reality may dispel the feelings of delight that inspire me when I read about such places or listen to travellers' tales, a delight never quite devoid of illusion. This is why I do not care for a journey to Switzerland or Italy, Meccas both of most ordinary tourists.[4]

Why did I choose Mont Blanc?

I would repeat what I have just said about the moral dispositions that lead each of us to select his own style of life, for it applies equally to our choice of travel. There, too, there must be independence of mind. I am among those who prefer the grandeur of natural landscapes to the sweetest or most charming views imaginable . . . and that is why I chose Mont Blanc. I would add that a very small number of travellers have ventured into these exalted regions, and that the curious accounts that several of them have given of their ascents do much to arouse and nurture my interest. Furthermore, women sometimes see and feel things very differently from men, and when I went to Mont Blanc it had not been ascended by any woman capable of remembering her impressions. One final consideration was that it was only fifty miles away, and, in such cases, proximity is indeed an advantage, for it lessens the fatigue and tedium of the journey while leaving the pleasure intact.

For how long had I had the idea?

As an idea, for ten years; as a plan, for a month; as a firm resolve, for a fortnight.

Why did you wait until the summer was so far advanced? . . . August would have been better than September, and you were at Chamonix then.

The fortnight that has elapsed between my resolve to go and my departure itself has not been too long for the preparations necessary to such an expedition. One does not attend the court of the King of the Alps in a silk dress and a gauze bonnet; this venture requires a plainer garb.

Why did you not delay your expedition until 1839?

In 1838, my will is stronger, I am more sure-footed, my first trip to the Alps – to Mont Joli and le Jardin – holds the promise of success for a bolder attempt. Who knows what 1839 may bring! . . . Ah, years, years! They are like days: they follow each other, but each is different.

These endless questions were not the only thorn in my flesh, for they were accompanied by the most alarming predictions: I would suffer the fate of Dr Hamel[5] – I would return with frost-bitten feet like the Count of Tilly[6] – My sight would be ruined for ever by such an expedition – Mont Blanc would bring about a recurrence of my previous palpitations of the heart – Once I had reached a certain height, I would need to breathe in three times for each breath – A blood vessel would burst in my chest, in which case I would have to come down, or die – The rarefied air would make blood spurt from my eyes, nose, and ears – Perhaps I would be struck by a storm en route – When I reached the top, it might well be swathed in cloud, and then my whole journey would have been in vain.

Then, people asked to see the costume that had been made for my climb; everyone declared, feeling the weight of it in their hands, that I could not walk for even half an hour so caparisoned!

Driven beyond endurance by these questions and gloomy predictions, I could see only one solution. I rang the bell: 'Jeannette[7], if anyone calls to see me, you will say that I am not at home.'

'And Mademoiselle's friends, am I to send them away, too?'

'There are to be no exceptions.'

After this I encountered no more opposition.

As for support, there was little enough:

Among my family, there was *one* who approved.

Among my friends, *one* more.

And of the twenty-five thousand inhabitants of Geneva, I could hope to name up to *three* more.

Grand total: *Five!*

And yet, since my attempt has been crowned with success, things are quite changed: what was once arrant folly has become an intrepid venture, immortalizing the name of the dauntless heroine; friends, relations, and perfect strangers never tire of asserting that this enterprise, unprecedented for a woman, would not be complete without an account for the general interest.

The heart is lightened and the spirit soothed by writing for friends and family; the pen moves fast, thoughts crowd upon one, newly-awakened memories are reborn in all their erstwhile freshness; and the conviction that your news, whatever it may be, will meet with interest and indulgence imbues your writing with a kind of gay abandon that makes up in charm what it lacks in elegance or correctness.

But how difficult it is to write naturally when one is conscious always of the public; sometimes, it is true, passionate admirers, but all too often the harshest of carping critics! . . . When I can offer no scientific observations as a result of my exploit, no account that can boast complete novelty (for several interesting reports have already appeared on the same subject), have no claim to special favour, and no clique to support me; when, in short, I am not only a woman but a country-woman to boot, what impertinence to say: here is my book.

And so I am writing for my family and friends, but not for the public.

I have been urged to believe that the public is not composed of those readers who hunt through a book in search of the faults that pepper it, and who take pleasure in picking them out or in puffing them up; that the tale of my journey is not an academic work, and that its content is by no means of purely literary interest; that if my account is truthful, my remarks simple and natural, the real public will realize this and turn a blind eye to those stylistic faults which would go uncensured in all but professional writers . . .

These reasons seem compelling to me, and so I will write and I will publish.

But in what form? On this subject I have encountered a welter of conflicting advice. One says: take up your pen at once, while your recollections are still vivid; another: give yourself time to see the expedition as a whole and to see what stands out from your first impressions; another: leave nothing out, recount all that you felt both physically and spiritually, for that will enliven your account; still another: beware, do not swamp the main story in a flood of trivial details, for the sure way to boredom is to tell all. Yet a fifth, a woman: take nobody's advice, above all a man's, for this tale must bear the feminine stamp. A sixth: Let your account sparkle, for this airy venture is almost a poem; do not give a flat, prosaic account. A seventh: Write as the spirit moves you, avoiding above all any pretension, any falsity, for then you will be true to yourself.

And it is this last piece of advice that I have followed, while profiting as best I can from the others. So, before putting pen to paper, I have allowed my thoughts to settle, although not so long as to consign to oblivion those first fresh impressions; I have set down all that I deemed of general interest, while keeping for myself those emotions which are too near and intimate to permit of general perusal. I will not resort to spurious sentiment, but if my imagination was sometimes stirred by the grandeur of the natural scene, why should I hesitate to admit to it?

So I take up my pen without a predetermined plan, but firm in my resolve to be both truthful and scrupulous in all I have to say. Perhaps this short narrative may not be altogether without interest for those who are already acquainted with these wonderful mountains, nor without its uses for those who might hope to visit them one day.

PART ONE

Before the Ascent

Chapter I

MY DEPARTURE FROM GENEVA

It was written in my stars that, for a short trip of fifty miles, I should suffer as many tribulations as have often deterred those who embark on much longer journeys. I had eluded advice, sermons and predictions by simply refusing visitors; and yet my most relentless opponent was to prove the weather. For eight days on end the rain teemed down! . . . I was sure that what fell as rain at Geneva must be snow at Mont Blanc, thus impairing my chances of success. Even had I wished to pretend otherwise, I could not have done so, because in the brief interludes when a ray of sunshine parted the clouds, I would hasten to Rousseau's Island to observe the state of the mountains,[1] only to find that they were covered with snow, not merely on their summits, but also half-way down. If I caught sight of the top of Mont Blanc towering over this snowy landscape, I was thrown into a condition that I now find hard to comprehend or to explain: my heart beat furiously, my breathing was impeded, and deep sighs burst from my breast. I felt such a burning desire to climb that an allied impulsion throbbed in my feet, and the mere thought of delaying the ascent to the following year plunged me into an inexpressible physical and moral distress . . . When, on my return from these walks, I met friends or acquaintances who said triumphantly: 'Well! Is that the end of your great plans? You cannot go up this year now!', these words caused me a deep and private pain. I came home fatigued and agitated, could neither eat nor sleep, and spent a night of agony, listening to the rain lashing the shutters. But, not before time, my torments came to an end: the sun shone again at last, and with it hope revived.

Worn down by the nervous prostration to which I had been

brought by uncertainty, I wrote to the head of the Society of Guides at Chamonix to tell him of my planned ascent.[2] I asked him to warn Joseph-Marie Couttet that I was hiring him as overall leader of my Mont-Blanc expedition, and I also charged him with retaining five other guides whom I named as companions. Finally I assured him that I was only waiting for his answer to set off.

I went also to see my doctor, Monsieur C., to tell him of the various precautions, sartorial and otherwise, that I had taken, and I requested him to indicate what measures I should take to safeguard my health before and during the ascent. To salve his conscience, he insisted on saying a few words about the danger inherent for a woman in such an undertaking. I interrupted him thus: 'Doctor, my mind is made up!' Endowed with as much tact as skill, he at once realized that it would be not only useless but impertinent to pursue the matter further, and confined himself to giving me the advice I sought. Moreover, he had the goodness to promise that he would leave all other engagements at once to answer any summons from me, should an accident force me to call upon his talents. All my life I shall remember his offer with gratitude.

I set my private affairs and papers in perfect order, and then went to procure my passport; these tasks left me more composed, because they were furthering my cherished ambition.

For me, the worst in all things, be they small or large, is uncertainty. My disposition is such that prolonged apprehension of any difficulty, set-back, or misfortune is, for me, more debilitating than the occurrence itself, however dreadful if may be! The continual see-sawing between hope and fear dissipates the strength of mind that brings resignation after the event.

I was waiting for an answer from the head guide at Chamonix when, in the evening of the 29th of August I was told that the Sardinian Consul had called to see me, on vital business. As you can imagine, I lifted my previous embargo on visitors; and indeed, Monsieur de M. had come to tell me that five Englishmen were leaving the next day for an ascent of Mont

Blanc. He told me that he had issued them with passports that very day, and added that he had not wanted to leave me in ignorance of this circumstance, believing that I should know of it, not only to ensure first choice of guides, but, if I so desired, to elect to make my own ascent on the same day, but a little later, following the trail they had blazed. I thanked the Consul for this kindly warning; as soon as he left I began to pack my trunks, and continued into the night. In the morning I went to bid farewell to my friends, and sent out for a comfortable, light carriage to take me as far as Saint-Martin. We settled a price for a little barouche with a good horse, and, at the agreed time, there appeared at my door the most paltry of dog-carts and the most broken-down of nags. I nearly refused this miserable substitute, but, quite apart from the delay it would have incurred, the driver gave me such a glowing account of the virtues of his animal, and promised so faithfully that it would get me to Saint-Martin in less than eight hours, that in the end I believed him. So, my effects were placed on the carriage; I installed myself in the carriage, not without difficulty, and Jeannette joined me; we set off, to a chorus of good wishes from a disapproving crowd.

Chapter II

BONNEVILLE CASTLE

At the beginning of the journey all went well; the poor old horse fairly galloped along! I was full of admiration for its powers, and said as much to its master, who plumed himself as he reiterated: 'Did I not tell you so? Although she is twenty years old, she can still hold her own with all the best horses.' We reached Bonneville in four hours, and such was my pleasure and gratification that I ordered the driver to reward her with a double ration of oats.

I made good use of the two-hour halt by visiting the castle at Bonneville, now a prison; the concierge showed me all there was to see. As he led me to the towers, he told me that in the depths of one of them lay a prisoner condemned to death.

The idea that I was only a few steps away from some unfortunate creature who was soon to be torn from society drove me to exclaim: 'Great Heavens! What crime has he committed, then?'

'I cannot tell you, but would you like to ask him yourself?'

'Oh, no, no! What could I find to say to him, as his end is so near?'

'Not as near as that! He still has another three months to live.'

'Three months to wait after being condemned to death!!! That is worse than death itself.'

To my horror, the fellow burst out laughing; but the joke was explained soon enough when he turned the key in the lock and the door swung open on its hinges. Then I saw . . . the ugliest of beasts, lying on a little straw and grunting gently, and my compassion was turned to amusement.

I must confess that this little trick was not in the best of taste, but I learnt that it had duped a number of travellers, and consoled myself with the thought that I was by no means the only one to have been caught out in this way.

I made my way to my hotel and, after a light meal, set out once more, revelling in the prospect of miraculous progress, as a result of the double measure of oats, and of a feather in my cap over the nine Englishmen.

But scarcely had we gone half a mile from Bonneville, when the poor old horse started to flag: her trot became a walk, and her walk a stop. The use of the whip restored the same three speeds: trot, walk, stop, and so on, all the way to the Café at Balme, where I paused on my own account to honour the grotto with a cannon shot;[1] the grotto returned the compliment with a thunderous rumbling. I cannot tell whether it was these unaccustomed sounds that finished off the poor beast's legs for good, but from that moment on there was no more trotting. All she could manage was a snail's pace, varied by a rest every five minutes! In vain did we get down from the carriage and walk, in the hope of lightening her load; nothing could hasten our progress.

'So, much to my chagrin, I am proved right, am I not?' I said to my driver. 'Indeed, it seemed from the first that such a miserable old nag would never have strength enough to get us there, poor skinny thing!'

'But you saw how she went as far as Bonneville?'

'Yes, but look how she's going now: at this rate, we shall not reach Saint-Martin till nightfall.'

'That's all we need, for it's no more than ten minutes from there to Sallanches, where we shall stop for the night.'

'You may, but I shan't; I am determined to continue on my way to Chamonix, and I had hoped to cover the bad roads by day.'

'They have improved the roads not long since, including the Nant Noir; now two carriages may pass together. Besides, there's a fine, bright moon tonight, and if you want to continue to Sallanches instead of stopping at Saint-Martin, I will undertake to get you there.'

This promise endowed me with a quite uncharacteristic

degree of patience; not another grumble passed my lips, and I even called a halt for a few minutes opposite the Nant d'Arpenas.

This waterfall, swollen by the rain that had thrown me into such despair at Geneva, was magnificent, and all the more so when viewed by moonlight. Set in all the wonderful austerity of the landscape that still lay between us and Sallanches, it evoked in me a mood of romance that inspired the sweetest reveries, which were, however, rudely interrupted by the words 'Here we are'. We had reached Sallanches and were just entering the courtyard of the Bellevue hotel, owned by Master Lafin. It was about half-past six.

Relying on the promise made by my driver, I was expecting to continue on my way immediately, but this was not to be. The greed of the hoteliers led them to all kinds of machinations to prevent this simple plan, they even went so far as to invent regulations which did not exist. Unjust demands culminated in insults and even threats.

My readers will readily understand why I pass over the details of this unedifying scene, in which the whole rabble of the inn took part. Suffice it to say that the general conspiracy, to force me willy-nilly into a night under Master Lafin's roof, or into the hire of horse and carriage at a scandalous rate,[2] was only circumvented by my own implacability. I spent the night in the carriage and thus frustrated this vulgar intrigue.

I feel it my duty to record such impositions, in the interest of future travellers: to set up a warning light on a reef where I was nearly wrecked and so save them from a similar fate.[3]

Chapter III

MY ARRIVAL AT CHAMONIX

I left as dawn was breaking, and within four hours the most diligent of postillions ensured my arrival at Chamonix. My very first preoccupation was to hurry to find the leader of the Society of Guides, in order to retain the services of those I most trusted before the Englishmen should forestall me. He told me that they had had no word of the latter, and that, acting on my letter from Geneva, he had sent to his cousin Couttet, instructing him to speak to the five other guides I had indicated.

With my mind thus set at rest about the possibility of forfeiting my advantage, I made my way to Joseph Couttet's little shop, but was sorry to find he was not there; he had just left to take some travellers to the Montanvert. I enquired for Pierre-Joseph Simond (my guide for le Jardin), but he had gone to Martigny the day before, and was not to return till the evening. His cousin, David Simond, was doing the walk around Mont Blanc. Mathieu Balmat was going up the Flégère and David Folliguet, up the Brévent; as for François Desplan, he was leading another group. Thus, of the six guides requested in my letter, none was at Chamonix. Imagine my impatience, doomed as I was to uncertainty till evening came. I planned to begin the ascent the very next morning, and little enough remained of that day for the preparations for such an expedition. I demanded the best room on the first floor of the hotel; it was engaged, but I was promised it in a few hours. The difficulties I encountered at every turn deprived me of appetite and sleep, even though the night of starvation and insomnia I had spent in my carriage at Sallanches ought to have ensured them both.

At last I was told that my room had been vacated. I went up to install myself and hardly had I made my dispositions when Couttet appeared. He had just learnt of my arrival, and already knew, from my Geneva letter, what was my intention in returning to Chamonix. As soon as I saw him, I gave him my hand: 'Well, my good man, here is a lady to offer you a tenth ascent.[1] Will you fail her?'

'No, truly,' he replied, 'I promised to lead your expedition if ever you decided to undertake it.[2] I will keep to my word and I will go, even though this is not really the best time because of the snow.'

'Sit down and let us discuss all this. Have you spoken to the five other guides I asked for in my letter?'

'Yes, except for David Simond who has left to take a walker round Mont Blanc, and who will not be back for three days. I will tell him when he returns.'

'What can you mean, "when he returns"? I cannot think we will wait three days to begin the ascent, for I intend to leave tomorrow, if you think we have time for the necessary preparations.'

'Tomorrow! Out of the question! You could never arrange for the provisions in what is left of today, for we must not go hungry up there. In any case, the guides you chose are all elsewhere.'

'They are all returning this evening, except for David Simond, whose place can be taken by another; as for the food, they can stay up all night to prepare it if necessary.'

'Ah, but you're forgetting it's Sunday tomorrow, which is another difficulty; no one will want to set out on a Sunday.'

'Then I will go and ask permission from the curé, and I am sure he will not refuse, for he knows how important it is to profit by good weather for such an expedition.'

'It's not certain he will agree, nor that my colleagues will want to profit. *You* talk to them; perhaps they will consent, though they never would to me, I know.'

'Ah! Heavens! Two more days of waiting! Well, I shall try to cut short this torment. Go and find any guides that may have returned and bring them to me!'

Couttet went out, and was soon back with François Desplan, and the next moment my worthy le Jardin guide, Pierre-Joseph Simond, appeared. We needed to choose a substitute for David Simond; the vote went to Anselme Tronchet – all were loud in his praises. So I accepted him as the sixth guide and was introduced to him, as well as to Balmat and Folliguet. They were unanimous in agreeing that it was impossible to leave the next day and that, in any case, as the new snow must still be soft, and not yet bonded with the old, a delayed departure would give us a better chance.

Having the whole of Saturday to wait, I avoided the delicate subject of a Sunday departure, for I did not want to give these good people time to find excuses between the promise and the act of going. I therefore postponed my attack till the next day, and devoted the rest of Friday to beginning the little journal which I was intending to keep throughout my journey.

As I had expected, this catalogue of frustrations culminated in a sleepless night.

Chapter IV

THE WAGER I MADE WITH JULIAN DEVOUASSOUD

The next morning, all Chamonix knew that a French lady had arrived to make the ascent. The natives of the valley regard Mont Blanc with such awe that they did not credit that a woman aspiring to conquer it could be in full possession of her senses. Some thought I would go no further than the Bossons glacier, others, that I would reach the first really deep crevasse; the wisest reckoned that the Grands Mulets would be my Pillars of Hercules. They were all convinced that, even if I succeeded in surmounting them, the great quantity of snow that lay beyond would spell catastrophe for me and all my companions. I discovered that Julien Dévouassoud, one of the most experienced guides in the valley, had engaged himself publicly, for a wager of *a thousand francs* against *a hundred sols*, that the ascent would not be completed, or would end in tragedy if I persisted in my intention.[1] The old head guide spoke to me of his trepidations with tears in his eyes and in a voice choked with emotion. Indeed, there was a general chorus of gloomy predictions; for myself, I was not in the least disturbed by them, for my mind was made up! To abandon my attempt rather than to abide by it would have needed much greater courage than I could boast. However, I was alarmed by the responsibilities inherent in taking the fathers of six families up Mont Blanc, and decided forthwith to take steps to cover myself. I therefore called together those of my guides who were at Chamonix that day, acquainted them with the sinister forebodings that had been expressed to me, and added that if they shared the general apprehension, it was better by far to forgo the undertaking than to embark on it while fearing some calamity. As far as I was concerned, I was determined to go through with it, and would therefore much prefer a withdrawal at Chamonix to a dereliction en route.

Those I spoke to expressed their determination to follow me to the summit, if my legs proved ready and willing to carry me so far. I enjoined Couttet to tell those who were absent that I was offering to release them from their promise, and why. At first, they replied that they would keep faith as their companions had done; but then, two hours later, Mathieu Balmat excused himself on the grounds of migraine, to be followed an hour later by David Folliguet, who claimed to fear cold too greatly to venture on Mont Blanc in the month of September. And yet they were stout fellows enough, Balmat and Folliguet; their oustanding qualities as guides, their courage, and their presence of mind figure largely in the fascinating account Mr Atkin has given of *his* ascent. I was sorry to lose them, but, in truth, I was not discomposed by this double defection, a sterner warning than any speeches of the dangers that were in store for me.

Who shall take their places? was my only question, and it was soon answered: Jacques Simond offered to replace Balmat, and Michel Favret came forward instead of Folliguet. I accepted these two guides, recommended as they were by their colleagues, and rejected several others who volunteered later. My party was complete.

Now, however, I had to persuade these good fellows to set out on a Sunday. I assembled them to make this suggestion, and saw by their clouded expressions, by the glances they exchanged, and by the total silence that ensued how distasteful this arrangement would be to them. But I persisted; sensible of their views, I added quickly, 'It goes without saying that we shall ask the curé's permission, that we shall hear Mass before leaving, and that we shall commend ourselves to the prayers of the faithful.'

'But there has been such a terrible precedent here, with Dr Hamel! . . . Ah, surely we cannot have forgotten him so soon!'

'What is the connection between that calamity and our departure on Sunday?'

'Do you not know that it was on Sunday, the 20th of August, 1820 *while High Mass was actually being said* that the dreadful accident took place, when the travellers fell almost at the summit and three of our men lost their lives? . . . If we ignored such a warning and set out on a Sunday, we should be defying the Almighty!'

'I have heard other reasons for this mishap than those you give, my friends. I do not wish to confront the divine anger any more than you do; but by taking the correct precautions, we shall not only be avoiding a sin, we shall act in accordance with our duty, by ensuring the best possible chances for an expedition where a misapprehension of the weather is a question of life and death.'

'Ah, what will people say? We should be cursed!'

'If we succeed, everyone will say that we were quite right to go; if we perish, we shall not hear the imprecations that you tell me will greet our misfortune.'

'On Monday, we are ready to leave as early as you will, but Sunday is out of the question! It would be blasphemous and that would bring bad luck.'

Couttet, for his part, opined that a delay of twenty-four hours would be advantageous, as it would give the new snowfalls time to settle.

I reiterated that conditions would be ideal if we left on Sunday – five whole days of good weather, with the barometer set fair (an earnest of three more) – and that twenty-four hours more for the snow to settle did not seem to me a sufficient recompense for the appalling possibility of a change in the weather once we were actually on Mont Blanc. But in vain; all my logic was powerless against the recollection of the tragic expedition of 1820. Opposition was unanimous; there was nothing for it but to yield and to postpone our departure till Monday.

To escape the myriad recommendations and predictions that I anticipated, I spent much of the day engaged upon my little journal, but I could not avoid them at dinner. Everyone tried to dissuade me from my intention by detailing the disadvantages – the certain dangers – without allowing the possibility of success. Many of the company had already retired, and I was on the point of doing so myself, when an English lady, my neighbour during dinner, turned quickly to me and embarked on the following conversation.

'Madam, although I only made your acquaintance twenty-four hours ago, you have aroused in me so lively an interest that I feel it incumbent on me to reveal the truth, a truth which everybody has implied, but none has dared express frankly. To be brief, if you set out for Mont Blanc with such risks against you, two to one you will never return.'

'Madam,' I replied, 'while I am grateful to you for the concern that lies behind this terrible prediction, allow me, if you please, not to take it too literally, for your claim is invalidated by the mere fact that I have found six experienced guides who are ready to accompany me.'

'They are unwilling to confess their fears to you, or perhaps they will not admit them to themselves. But I must warn you that all those who are well acquainted with Mont Blanc are convinced that the great quantities of snow that fell a week or ten days ago will prevent an ascent, or at least make it dangerous in the extreme. They all say that you will suffer the fate of Dr Hamel!'

'Dr Hamel again! . . . I am dogged by his example, which everybody quotes against me even though it was the only fatal attempt! Yet my instinct tells me that I shall succeed, that no misfortune will mar this expedition, and that I shall return with wonderful memories.'

'But suppose that your instinct is wrong, and you fall into a crevasse or are swept away by an avalanche! . . .'

'I must take my chance of that! And if the worst comes to the worst, I will not be perturbed at the prospect of a tomb of ice.'

'Then you have no family, that you can talk so?'

'Yes, indeed I do; but if I were obsessed by the idea of losing them for ever, I should never do anything; I should not even venture out in a high wind for fear of being struck on the head by a falling tile. It is better to forget such thoughts when contemplating an undertaking such as mine: better to hope, as I do.'

'But those fathers you are taking with you: are you not alarmed by the responsibility of possible accident where they are concerned?'

'I warned them of public gossip and allowed all those who feared the outcome to withdraw from their commitment. I urged every man to follow his own convictions without being swayed by self-esteem. So you see, I am in no way responsible, as they know the country better than I do, they are coming of their own free will, and I am running the same risks as they.'

'But pray consider: in the two hours you allowed your guides to reconsider, two took the opportunity to resign.'

'True. But five others came forward to take their place. So . . .!'

'Well, Madam, I see that your mind is made up and I will not persist. If some misfortune should strike your expedition to Mont Blanc, I should reproach myself for the rest of my life for concealing the truth from you at a time when it might have prevailed. Now you know it, and are undaunted. All that remains now is to assure you of my wish, dearer to none than me, that your boldness may be crowned with the glory you seem to expect. If I have a regret, it is that I am not able to prolong my visit to Chamonix long enough to be the first to congratulate you if you are successful.'

I shook the hand of this excellent woman, much moved by an insistence that revealed the extreme goodness of her heart, but which was powerless against the strength of my determination.

In general, a decision should be preceded by reflection, by consultations with those friends and relations whose advice one values, and by a careful scrutiny of all aspects of the plan, giving particular attention to the disadvantages; but once one's mind is made up, everything but the advantages should be forgotten and one should remain fixed in one's intentions, unmoved by the praise or blame of the world. Otherwise life would be frittered away in every kind of uncertainty and doubt.

I returned to my chamber and reflected on all that had just been said to me, without being in the least discomfited by it; nevertheless, the nature of the prophecies, which everyone seemed intent upon making as gloomy as possible, and above all the obligations which they laid at my door in case of accident, combined to rob me of the sleep I so much needed. I slept very little, very badly, and pondered much! . . . Just the contrary of what had been prescribed for me. But whose fault was that?

Chapter V

PREPARATIONS

When I opened my shutters on Sunday morning, I was greeted by the sight of the highest of mountains glowing in the most beautiful weather! Not a cloud between me and the summit I aspired to; the air was so clear that with the naked eye you could have seen a chamois leaping over the glaciers. It was, in short, one of those brilliant days which God sometimes sends travellers, when they cannot but think of Him and bless Him.

But can you imagine how immensely provoked I was when my guides refused to set off! Such perfect weather to begin my ascent! And who could convince me that the delay I was forced to accept would not incur a complete change? I remembered my recent expedition to Mont Joli, and was horrified at the mere thought that I might encounter the same weather on Mont Blanc, and reach the summit at the very moment when it became enveloped in cloud.

All my guides came to see me; I concealed my mortification and displayed only the confidence they inspired in me and my hopes of a perfect success. I kept Couttet back to discuss the provisioning of our little troupe.

'You told me one must not go hungry up there, my dear Couttet; well now, what shall we need? I intend to do everything aright, and I have not the slightest idea what we shall require in the course of our expedition.'

'Will you write?'

'Yes, you dictate.'

I took up my pen and he dictated as follows:

'On leaving, a good substantial breakfast for six guides, six porters, and the mule-driver. Then, to be put in the bags:

Two legs of mutton
Two sides of veal
Twenty-four roast chickens
Six loaves of three to four pounds each
Eighteen bottles of Saint-Jean
One of Cognac brandy
One of vinegar
One of fern-syrup
One small barrel of vin ordinaire for the porters' break at the Grands Mulets
Twelve lemons
Three pounds of sugar
Three pounds of chocolate
Three pounds of prunes
A good, hearty, reviving dinner on our return.'

'Is that all?'

'Yes, for us. But now, if you want anything particular for yourself, you should add it to the list.'

I wrote:

A blancmange
A flagon of barley water
A flagon of lemonade
A pot of chicken bouillon

As you will see, what I intended for my private consumption was hardly lavish. I took this list to the hotel cook, instructing him to have all ready at seven o'clock so that we could pack the bags that same evening and be free of little practical concerns the next morning.

After mass, I paid a visit to the curé; I knew he was much loved by his parishioners, and general affection must always speak well for a priest. This good man assured me of all his best wishes; I told him how greatly I had been mortified at losing a day of such splendid weather, and how I had tried in vain to persuade my guides to leave after mass, with his permission. 'I must confess,' he replied, 'that I would have given it only with the greatest reluctance, for in the event of some misfortune, guides and priest alike would have been blamed. But take heart, all will be well; we will ask God for His protection on all travellers and He will grant it.'

After speaking of the fortune, both good and bad, that might attend my exploit, I told the priest of my desire to take with me up Mont Blanc one of the pigeons from his dovecote, to discover how it would stand the high atmosphere and how long it would take to find its way back to Chamonix from the summit. My request was granted most graciously. We agreed that I would not collect the bird till I was on the point of departure, and that we would choose one of the oldest inhabitants of the dovecote, a father bird, which would be most likely to return. We also agreed that a watch would be kept for its arrival, and that this would be signalled to us by a white flag spread out on the ground beside the church.

Leaving the curé's house, I crossed the square which was filled with little clusters of people all whispering together; the air of disquiet which had struck me the previous day was even more noticeable on Sunday. On reaching the hotel, I discovered the cause of it. Despite adverse indications, two other expeditions were being organized for the same day as mine. One was to be led by a Polish traveller whose name I only discovered at the Grands Mulets, the other by Monsieur Eisenkraemer, a German resident at the Union Hotel. These two gentlemen were willing for anyone who volunteered to accompany them, so that Mont Blanc was threatened by a monstrous invasion of all the world and his wife! I was much comforted by the thought that if there were an accident, all these walkers could come to each other's aid. But although several guides expressed a desire to amalgamate all three parties into one, I absolutely refused, for I wanted to be alone with my own impressions during my trip; I was further moved by a sense of propriety which dictated that a woman travelling alone, unaccompanied by a male relation, could not, and should not, associate with strangers, even fortuitously.

I therefore warned my guides that I was proposing to set out alone and to keep my own party separate throughout the expedition, except at those points where a joint stopping-place was unavoidable, such as the rock at the Grands Mulets, which is the only possible bivouac in those deserted regions. And, as I had been told that there was one place to strike camp which was infinitely superior to all others, I declared that I intended to be the first to leave, in order to secure the best position in this novel caravanserai. We therefore settled that we should be woken at four o'clock, breakfast at five, and leave at six. Since this first day was to last no more than eight hours, including two by mule, there was no need to start out any earlier, even in order to forestall the two other parties, who were not due to leave until half-past six and seven o'clock respectively.

My readers will readily understand the renewed concern that spread through Chamonix on the news of this threefold ascent. Its object was not the three climbers; if it was their fancy, their whim, their caprice to go up Mont Blanc, so be it; if something 'went wrong', so much the worse for them! But twenty guides and volunteers were to accompany them; only think of the general anxiety, for from every family there would be a husband, a father, a son, or a brother in danger. Thus, despite the brilliant sunshine that flooded the valley, everyone insisted that fortune was all against us.

As for my guides, they were hopeful of success, as long (they said) as the weather remained fair and Mademoiselle's legs remained strong. I was able to reassure them on this last point, certain that they, at least, would not fail me when put to the test.

The reader will probably like to make closer acquaintance with the travellers whose path to the summit he will soon follow. The following chapters therefore contain a short account of each of them.

Chapter VI

SELF-PORTRAIT

Perhaps, before giving you a likeness of my guides, I should have sketched my own. Would it be a faithful one? That would be my intention, certainly, but I considered that since my personality would emerge naturally in the course of my narrative, I would allow the curious free rein to form a composite picture of the broad outlines of my character. I am sure you will realize that while I am happy to retail to the public a venture which has attracted some attention in the world, I cannot neglect that delicate sense of propriety which forbids a lady to draw her own portrait.

I therefore confine myself to satisfying the general curiosity with a faithful depiction of my features and of the costume I wore during my expedition.[1] I will say, as well, that when I made my ascent, I was four-and-forty years, five months, and twenty-four days old,[2] and that I was therefore by no means a *Young Frenchwoman*, as was reported in one newspaper,[3] nor even a *Lady of nearly forty*, as another newspaper had it.[4] In my position any other woman would have thanked them for their gallantry, but, in my capacity as historian of the truth, I insist on reclaiming the years they stole from me.

Chapter VII

MY GUIDES

Now I will introduce my guides to the reader.

Joseph-Marie Couttet, leader of my party: five-and-forty, small of stature, with an expression both witty and intelligent. He is one of the most famous Chamonix guides, a well-deserved reputation in view of his wide range of knowledge, which renders him entertaining as well as useful where travellers are concerned. This includes, first of all, his local knowledge, for there is not the smallest corner, not a plateau nor a point that he cannot name, no information that he cannot provide. He is at once a mineralogist, a botanist, and a shopkeeper. In summer, he practises as a guide and sells minerals in the various shops in Chamonix, Montanvert, and Les Ouches. In winter, he travels through the great cities, such as Milan, Lyon, and Geneva, engaged in a different form of trade. Since his diligence has been rewarded with success he has amassed a small fortune, which would allow him to live at ease were it not for the fact that the pleasure he takes in his work attaches him to the various concerns he has built up.

His only daughter is the sweet and graceful mountain-girl you may see at Montanvert, and he and his wife occupy a fine house that he has had built in the village of les Pèlerins. Near neighbour that he is, he is most closely acquainted with Mont Blanc. When I arrived at Chamonix, he was on his ninth ascent;[1] mine was his tenth successful sortie.

Anselme Tronchet: two-and-fifty, of distinguished appearance, due as much to his tall stature as to his gravity of speech and bearing. He was the eldest of our party, and although he had only climbed Mont Blanc once,[2] he enjoyed a firm reputation as an excellent guide. Simultaneously miller, carpenter, builder, roadmender, and stonemason, he needs all he earns to support his nine children. In this, he is ably partnered by the most hard-working of wives: it is she who works the two mills her husband owns, and who regrinds the millstones when necessary; she who wields pick, shovel, and needle and cares for the children; and she who seems to be everywhere at once, and will turn her hand to anything in the struggle to bring up her large family.

One little talent which I must not omit to mention here, because it makes Tronchet so valuable to artists, is the wonderful way he sharpens pencils. You give them to him blunt, and he returns them needle-sharp and shapely, so clean that you could write or draw in white gloves. This for the benefit of jotters and sketchers.

Jacques Simond: fifty, medium height, open expression. He excels in chamois-hunting, he is their deadliest enemy, and when he finds one, he can sell its skin even before bringing it down, and never fears the discomfiture of the man in the story. The walls of his house are lined with all the instruments of war: there you may see guns, carbines, ammunition pouches, powder-horns, nailed boots and great leather gaiters, all interspersed with the corpses of his victims. You realize what such a pastime, practised regularly, does to ensure a firm footing over rocks and glaciers.

Hunting is not the only occupation and talent of Jacques Simond; he is a tailor, and he clothes his two sons, and sometimes even his two little girls and his wife, for whom he makes aprons and hems fichus.[3] As a carpenter, he has made all the furniture in their simple home. He has attempted the ascent several times, but has succeeded only once;[4] however, this causes him no great concern, for he is beginning to find Mont Blanc somewhat high for his old legs, and the snow somewhat dazzling for his old eyes.

Pierre-Joseph Simond, my first guide at Chamonix: seven-and-forty, well-built, greying hair, a good honest face if ever there was one! and as steady on his feet in the middle of the glaciers as on the high road. He has already taken part in three ascents,[5] and although he swore that would be all, he agreed to this last one out of courtesy to the lady he took to le Jardin.

Simple, pious and steady, this good fellow tends his little plot, supplementing its fruits with what he earns as a guide; altogether, this yields a modest income that he divides among his wife and two children.

Michel Favret: two-and-forty, bearing grave and gentle, full of little attentions for the travellers he accompanies, a quality no doubt shared by all the splendid Chamonix guides, but possessed by him to an unusual degree.

Favret is so well-looked upon in these parts that it is almost always he who is entrusted with confidential business by the local administration. Like my five other guides, he is married with children, having a very pretty wife and three offspring. He has made three ascents of Mont Blanc and augments his earnings as a guide with the profits from small-scale sheep-trading.[6]

François Desplan: nine-and-thirty, height above the average, a most pleasing expression which betrays his candour and cheerfulness. The lightness and agility of a chamois, leaping crevasses as they do at a single bound. As stout a walker as he is a drinker when a halt is called. He is a hunter, but the annals of the chamois population report that he has not yet been responsible for many widows or orphans. He can sew, and performs many little feminine repairs when need arises. Apart from his profession as guide, he is also shoemaker, saddler, butcher, baker, carpenter, and chandler. He, too, is a dauntless climber who had already set foot seven times on the summit of Mont Blanc when I appeared to summon him for an eighth.[7]

He used to live in a little house at the foot of the Brévent, but he and his family were driven from it by an avalanche. Today, with nothing in the world apart from a wife, six daughters, and a dear little boy, all pink and chubby and worth a king's ransom, this genial fellow works, laughs, and sings his mountain life away without a care in the world. May God preserve him in such a happy state of cheerfulness, good health, and confidence in His providence.

These, then, were the six guides who were to share the perils of my trip to Mont Blanc. The many ascents they had already made, the experience they had thus gained, their manifest composure, all united to instil in me a perfect confidence and to make them, in my eyes, so many protectors to watch over my safety. With such companions, I would have gone to the end of the world.

And yet a shadow of guilt sometimes crossed my mind: if our little troupe were buried in an avalance, there would be, at a stroke, *six widows and twenty-seven orphans*!!!!

Chapter VIII

MY PORTERS

Properly speaking, the porters are the thirty additional guides from whom are recruited the principal guides, and at present I am not concerned with them, but with the helpers these same guides employ during ascents, who are also known as porters.

On such expeditions up Mont Blanc, the luggage becomes a real burden, for it comprises not only food for three days' march, but provision for the two bivouacs that must be made at the Grands Mulets, the extra clothing with which we were all equipped, and the instruments and little comforts that ordinarily accompany such travellers. It follows that it would be foolish for the guides to squander their strength on such porterage on the first day, instead of conserving it for the fourteen or fifteen hours' climbing the morrow. Each of them therefore allows himself one porter, whom he selects as seems best to him and sends back at whatever point suits him. The guide is responsible for paying the porter, but there is no law to prevent the traveller from displaying an appropriate generosity by adding to the modest fee that is the standard recompense for porters.

The six selected for my party were as follows: Joseph Simond, Michel Couttet, Pierre Balmat, Michel Tournier, Pierre Simond, and Jean Mugnier. The first four only went as far the the Grands Mulets, the other two to the summit. I will give my reader a short account of the latter, too, so that, knowing their previous history, you may be able to follow their exploits with greater interest.

Pierre Simond then: eight-and-thirty, a strong, healthy fellow with a robust constitution impervious to fatigue. Father of five young children, he, his large family, and his three unmarried sisters live in the little hamlet of Bois, near the source of the Arveiron. He has been a porter for four years, and has already completed all the important Alpine climbs: the Buet, le Jardin, the Col du Géant, the walk round Mont Blanc, and the ascent. Immune to sleepiness and the disorders usual at altitude, his slow, measured step is as steady going up as it is down, in mid-glacier as on a flat surface. If need arises, he can go beyond the call of duty to help or encourage the traveller,[1] and although not one of those entertaining guides who divert with their amusing tales and interest with their extensive knowledge, he is none the less a reliable, experienced companion, and entirely trustworthy.

Jean Mugnier: one-and-thirty, short, with a great domed forehead that shows his intelligence; yet his features, thin, pale, and timid as they are, in no way reflect the energy that abounds in him. He owns the little mill at Frasserend betwen Argentière and le Tour, and lives the mountain life there with his two sisters, both unmarried like him. To fill the gap between marriage and subsequent fatherhood, he has appointed himself head of the family and has adopted a young cousin and a little nephew, still a child, whom he is bringing up with a father's loving care. In the winter he is a miller, in the summer a porter, and, in addition, he is a mineralogist: thus, having acquired some practical knowledge of this science,[2] he explores the valley in the search for stone and minerals which he then sells to galleries.

Endowed with a scarcely credible degree of strength and courage, this fearless mountaineer does not hesitate to venture out alone on the huge Argentière glacier, and to remain there for days at a time with no other resources than a rope and an axe, scaling the steepest rocks and the deepest abysses. There, he spends his nights lying on the ice, right next to a crevasse and sometimes in the lee of an overhanging avalanche, and yet he sleeps peacefully on, as long as he has asked God to watch over him.

Unassuming in all his ways, this upright young man is unaware of his real value. Of exemplary religious habits, he believes he is merely doing his duty. In bringing up the children of his relations, he has no idea that he is acting generously.[3] While performing extraordinary feats of valour, it has never occurred to him that he is braver or worthier than the next man. He is ever ready to praise others, never to criticize . . . in a word, he is one of those untainted characters that have become increasingly rare in this civilized world of ours.

Chapter IX

MY LUGGAGE[1]

I will refrain from giving a detailed account of the emotions that assailed me on the eve of embarking on my great plan; suffice it to say that all the aggravations and delays that I have retailed here had imbued it with a sense of such urgency that I verily believe I would have scaled Mont Blanc alone rather than abandon the project. Although the general opinion of my venture had remained unchanged, people had finally come to realize that when someone has determined to undertake such an exploit and is on the verge of departure, vain remonstrances must give way to encouragement and good wishes. These were lavished upon me during that Sunday evening.

Eight o'clock was striking when my guides made their appearance; they had come to pack the baggage for our impending departure. The provisions were laid out on a great table and distributed so as to apportion the weight as equitably as possible. Then came the sheets, blankets, large and small ropes, saucepans, coal, bellows, stove – down to the very needles and thread. It was most instructive to see the skill and dispatch with which every article was folded, rolled, and tucked in where it best fitted. Couttet, above all, seemed to have perfected the art.

Several strangers were present at these preparations, among whom I noticed a gentleman and lady with whom I was unacquainted; but it was not hard to guess their provenance when they came up to me and, in a marked English accent, expressed their delight at finding themselves in Chamonix just when three ascents were to be made. Both of them imparted their best wishes for the success of my expedition; we were to meet later, at the foot of the mountain.

The guides asked for my personal baggage, in order to distribute it among themselves. I sent for it. My clothing consisted of:

Combinations of English flannel, to be worn next to the skin

A man's shirt, to be worn on top

A foulard cravat

Two pairs of silk stockings[2]

Two pairs of very thick woollen stockings

Two pairs of nailed boots, waterproof and of different sizes[3]

A pair of trousers, cut full, corded at the top, with gaiters at the bottom to tuck into the boots. These trousers were made of Scottish wool plaid with a warm, soft, fleece lining.

A blouse of the same material and lining, cut full, with tucks front and back to protect chest and back with six layers of wool.

A leather belt, arranged so as to sit rather low on the waist.

One pair of knitted gloves with a fur lining

One pair of gloves with the fur outside, large enough to fit over the others, with deep fur cuffs to keep out the air

A boa

A close bonnet of the same material as the blouse, lined as well, trimmed with black fur, and with a green veil attached to the brim[4]

A large straw hat from Chamonix, with a green lining and four strings to hold it firmly in place[5]

A black velvet mask

A long stick with a ferrule

A plaid

A pelisse, fur-lined throughout, for the night and the coldest part of the day.

This costume, as I wore it from the Grands Mulets onwards, weighed fourteen full pounds (counting just one pair of boots), and the pelisse and plaid that I put on at some points weighed another seven pounds (making twenty-one pounds in all).

Apart from these garments, essential for the conditions we would encounter, I also took several articles which added to the comfort and convenience of the journey, to wit:

A large, flat, straw basket, well-lined, and equipped with small inside pockets

A phial of vinegar salts

A phial of eau-de-Cologne

An enormous fan, in case I had to be given air

A small one, to fan myself

A folding pocket-knife

A shoehorn, for changing my boots

A small spirit kettle, to make tea in five minutes, or to heat soup

Inside this kettle, a flask of alcohol

A composition box containing tea

A similar box containing cucumber pomade

A tinder-box

A thermometer, to measure the varying degrees of cold

A first-class telescope[6]

Two flannel towels

A friction brush, in case of numbness

A rubber pillow

Two flasks, with their own beakers, one containing almond milk and the other lemonade

The indispensable notebook, with half-a-dozen sharp pencils

Finally, a small looking-glass, a truly feminine *article, which I would none the less recommend most strongly to anyone contemplating an expedition at altitude (even a captain of dragoons!). For one may use it to examine the skin to see what ravages the mountain air has wrought, and remedy them by*

> *rubbing gently with cucumber pomade, before a blister warns, too late, alas!, of precautions overlooked or forgotten. And if some uncharitable reader still persists in believing that this article was for beauty and not utility, I can only castigate him for such foolishness. For one's vanity suffers so severely in the bitter cold of the Mont-Blanc climate that I would have preferred to remain in ignorance till we returned to the valley.*

Once the bag were packed, I had only to follow my guides' advice, to go to bed and to recoup the sleep I had missed the two previous nights, not to mention what I needed for that night and the two sleepless nights that were likely to follow. I did try, but in vain . . .! So I occupied the hours before departure by writing letters to my nearest and dearest, which were only to be delivered if some dreadful misfortune should strike. Since I could not exclude the possibility of an *accident*, I wrote a note to the good Dr C., reminding him of the promise he had made. All these I enclosed with instructions for my maid, enjoining her to send this packet to the post at Sallanches if I perished, that letter express to Geneva if I should break an arm or a leg, and to keep all safe if, as I hoped, I returned unscathed.

As I penned the last line, I felt my head nodding and my eyes closing . . . I sprang to my bed, quickly snuffed the candle, and fell into the deepest sleep I had had for many a day. It was then half-past one.

PART TWO

During the Ascent

Chapter X

OUR DEPARTURE FROM CHAMONIX FOR THE ASCENT

How sweetly I was sleeping when I was awakened by two or three loud thumps on my door, followed by Couttet's voice saying: 'Mademoiselle, it is four o'clock, you must get up.' I would as soon have heard the lugubrious exhortation of the Trappists: 'Brother, we must all die', as this summons from my head guide, shattering as it did the first real sleep I had enjoyed for days. Nevertheless, I sprang from my bed with alacrity! And yet the effort of this first victory cost me almost as dear as my conquest of Mont Blanc itself.

I was soon dressed, and came downstairs to review my troops: all were duly drawn up for inspection, my six guides in full mountain rig, the six porters, and the mule-driver.[1] Despite the early hour, the hotel balconies were already crowded with curious spectators, and small groups of people were clustered about the square, waiting to witness our departure. The weather promised magnificently: the sky was of a perfect serenity, the barometer remained set fair. The guides seemed composed, but I could not be: I was filled with an uncontrollable joy, my body felt light as air, being neither hot nor cold, hungry nor thirsty; only it was drawn so strongly towards Mont Blanc that, had I given it free rein, it would have rushed up at full speed. I could not wait to set out, and forced myself to delay until the time agreed by inspecting the breakfast; I found that it was substantial indeed, just as Couttet had requested.

I urged my party to take their seats, and stopped a moment to watch them eat: it was gratifying to see how rapidly these thirteen men of the mountains disposed of enormous slabs of meat. If anything could have given me an appetite at such a time, it would have been their example. It goes without saying that, as you might expect, they drank to the health of the lady and the success of the trip. The said lady, in recognition of this and seeing that all was well, retired to her own room for a few minutes.

And so the longed-for moment had come at last! I was about to survey nature's grandest vistas! I was conscious that I should be worthy the contemplation of all the poetry and splendour they had to offer. It was not the puny fame of being the first woman to venture on such a journey that filled me with the exhilaration such projects always call forth; rather, it was the awareness of the spiritual well-being that would follow. This one memory would counterbalance many others less welcome. Happy a thousand times those who are not impelled to flee the disillusion of life's trivial round and to seek refuge in fantasy!

On the very threshold of this perilous expedition, I raised my eyes to Him who orders the success and failure of all things, and a short but fervent prayer rose from my heart rather than my lips! . . . And it was heard indeed, since my enterprise was blessed with a favourable issue, nor was it marred by an accident of any kind.

I was informed that all were ready and waiting; I joined them and found that all was prepared for departure, except that we had forgotten the pigeon. It was quickly fetched from the curé, while I took a reading from my thermometer. Pointing to the north, it registered six above zero (Réamur[2]). I then took my pulse, being eager to record the variations it might undergo as the journey proceeded. It was beating at sixty-four to the minute (four beats more than usual[3]).

At last our fifteenth traveller, the pigeon, appeared; six o'clock struck: our signal to be off. I embraced my poor Jeannette who promptly burst into floods of tears, received the farewells of the strangers thronging the veranda, and set out, with their good wishes ringing in my ears.

Those who saw our party on its way through the valley assured me that it looked very well. For this first part, I was clad in a dress of brown merino and white trousers; on my head sat a

Henriette d'Angeville.
(Miniature by Henriette Rath, 1830)

The Château of Lompnes, Ain:
Henriette d'Angeville's family home.

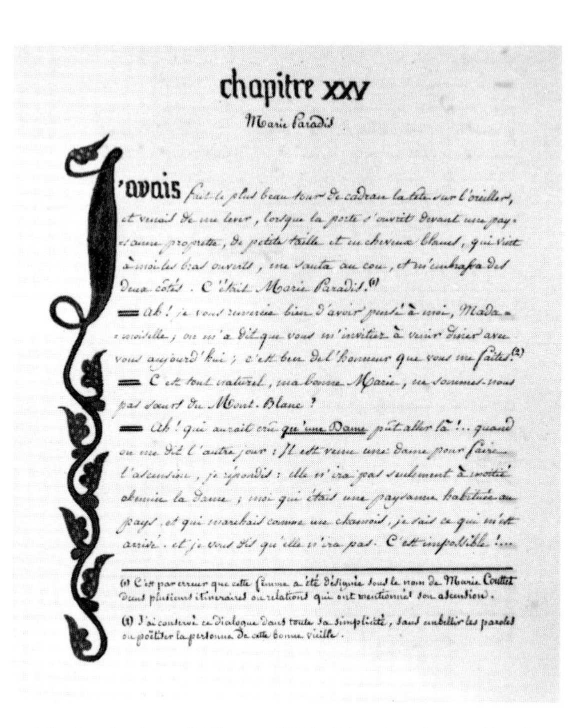

chapitre XXV

Marie Paradis

J'avais fait le plus beau tour de cadran la tête sur l'oreiller, et venais de me lever, lorsque la porte s'ouvrit devant une paysanne proprette, de petite taille et en cheveux blancs, qui vint à moi les bras ouverts, me sauta au cou, et m'embrassa des deux côtés. C'était Marie Paradis.(1)

— Ah! je vous remercie bien d'avoir pensé à moi, Mademoiselle; on m'a dit que vous m'invitiez à venir dîner avec vous aujourd'hui; c'est bien de l'honneur que vous me faites.(2)

— C'est tout naturel, ma bonne Marie, ne sommes-nous pas sœurs du Mont-Blanc?

— Ah! qui aurait cru qu'une Dame pût aller là!.. quand on me dit l'autre jour: Il est venu une dame pour faire l'ascension, je répondis: elle n'ira pas seulement à moitié chemin la dame; moi qui étais une paysanne habituée au pays, et qui marchais comme un chamois, je sais ce qui m'est arrivé. et je vous dis qu'elle n'ira pas. C'est impossible!...

(1) C'est par erreur que cette femme a été désignée sous le nom de Marie Couttet dans plusieurs itinéraires ou relations qui ont mentionné son ascension.

(2) J'ai conservé ce dialogue dans toute sa simplicité, sans embellir les paroles ou poétiser la personne de cette bonne vieille.

The beginning of Chapter 25 in Henriette's own hand.

Marie Paradis. *(Portrait by Henri Deville)*

Henriette d'Angeville in her mountaineering costume.
(Watercolour by Jules Hébert)

Chamonix and Mont Blanc.
(This illustration is from Henriette's own Album)

The Union Hotel. *(From Henriette's own Album)*

Departure. *(Pencil sketch by Jules Hébert)*

The Porters. *(Watercolour by Henri Deville)*

The Guides. *(Watercolour by Henri Deville)*

At the Bossons Glacier. Henriette d'Angeville, aided by Tronchet and Desplan, crossing small crevasses of two to three feet. *(Pencil sketch by Jules Hébert)*

An ice crête on the Bossons Glacier. *(Pencil sketch by Jules Hébert)*

On the ice wall.
(Pencil sketch by Jules Hébert)

On the Summit. 'You must go higher than Mont Blanc.' *(Pencil sketch by Jules Hébert)*

Triumphal Return. *(Pencil sketch by Jules Hébert)*

The Guides' Dinner at the Union Hotel. *(Watercolour by Henri Deville)*

little hat of light straw with a gauze veil, and the traditional staff was in my hand. Beside me walked my head guide, and in our wake came the twelve other mountaineers. My feet seemed winged – I scarcely walked, I ran! . . . 'Slowly, slowly!' cried the guides. 'Think of tomorrow.'

'My friends,' I replied from the front, 'once we are really on the mountain, you will be masters and decide everything; but till we reach the foot of Mont Blanc, I am the general and you the troops.'

We quickly reached the foot of the mountain, where I relinquished my command in favour of the guides, acknowledging their supremacy, promising to heed their advice and obey their instructions. The first sign of their authority was to put me up on to Moussa.

Now Moussa was a splendid beast, doyenne of the Chamonix mules, for she boasted four-and-twenty years in all, of which twenty had been devoted to duty! Recalling the creature I had been blessed with on my first trip,[4] more like a giraffe than a mule, I had urged the choice of an animal that was both steady and sure-footed, and these two qualities were combined in Moussa; indeed, the latter virtue was amply demonstrated by the dear creature's ascent to the Pierre-Pointue, completed without falling or stumbling! I hereby award her due credit for this achievement, for I set out for the summit as comfortable on her back as in my own armchair, as she climbed slowly, gently, and in perfect safety. Furthermore, she enabled me to conserve my energies and my legs for the time when they should be my only support.

We came to a chalet near the Pèlerins wood, and I had a sudden fancy to taste the local bread; one of the guides went in and returned with a kind of granite, which it was impossible even to get my teeth into. It was a solid slab of hard, black crust, which no well-bred dog would have looked at twice. I enquired whether this revolting fare was commonplace in those regions, and was astounded to learn that, almost without exception, people managed on it well enough. I sent up a private prayer of thanks to the Almighty, who had seen fit to set me in the middle station of life, rather than oblige me to earn such bread by the sweat of my brow.

Such an exact description of the terrain as far as the beginning of the Bossons glacier may be found in the accounts of my precursors on Mont Blanc, that I have nothing new to add to what they have said. I will simply reiterate that 'once you have reached the Pèlerins wood, the landscape becomes desolate in character; uprooted trees, deep ravines, and huge blocks of granite that have tumbled even to here, all bear witness to the furious violence of the swollen water-courses that leave such devastation in their track.'

Nor will I enter into a detailed dscription of the arid, rock-strewn regions that lead to the Pierre-Pointue; I will only say that when I reached it, I dismounted from my dear, steady Moussa and began to make my way up the mountain with all the facility of a practised mountaineer. For a long time, we followed a rocky arête along the top of a precipice; I amused myself by walking as close to the abyss as I could, peering over the edge and dropping stones into the depths below – a harmless enough pastime which was soon indulged in by the whole party. From there on, the guides and porters began to gather up any wood and dry twigs they could find, and to bundle them up ready for the camp-fire. Soon we had crossed the ground that lay between the Pierre-Pointue and the Pierre de l'Echelle, and reached this first stopping-point when Couttet's watch showed ten o'clock precisely.

Chapter XI

THE PIERRE DE L'ECHELLE

The bags were soon unfastened, and while the provisions required for the party's luncheon were being extracted, the guides made a soft seat for me with the covers from the baggage, where they made me rest. They laid a sheepskin under my feet, suggested that I should wear my shawl for the whole halt, and only considered their own needs and desires when they had attended to my own.

As soon as I had taken my seat, I instructed the thermometer to be placed facing north; it registered four degrees above zero, and maintained this level for the three-quarters of an hour we spent at the Pierre de l'Echelle. I also took my pulse when I judged that the agitation occasioned by the climb had abated, and found it read seventy-two to the minute. Having satisfied my curiosity on these two points, I turned my attention to contemplating the landscape which lay before me.

Opposite us rose the Brévent, on which a swarm of curious spectators could be distinguished with the aid of the telescope; further off, the Aiguilles Rouges, surmounted by the top of the Buet; still further, the Dents du Midi de Bex, and in the distance Mount Fénétral; to our left, the Bossons glacier, dominated by the Aiguille du Goûter; below lay the Col de Voza, the Prarion, and the Aravis range. At our feet, down in the valley, the view dropped sharply to the villages of les Pèlerins and les Praz far below.

The austerity of this panorama by no means detracted from its beauty.

I was busy recording all these names in my little notebook, when loud exclamations were heard: 'Look! There's one!'

'I can see two.'

'And I can see three.'

'Oh, if only I had my gun, and they were closer!'

'What is it?' I enquired, looking in the general direction.

'White grouse.'[1]

'Where are they? I have never seen them before.'

They pointed out the spot, and I observed the birds, first with the naked eye, and then with remarkable clarity with the telescope, as they strutted around on a rock not far from us, although out of range of the guns. When I had satisfactorily established their identity, and taken notes on them, my thoughts turned to luncheon, even though I still had no appetite. But I did eat, against future pangs, a wing of chicken, a tiny piece of bread, and two spoonsful of blancmange. The guides made a heartier repast: they soon disposed of a leg of mutton and drained three or four bottles, which they sent rolling down the mountainside like so many stones.

It was a pretty scene as we rested there at the foot of the rock. M. Eisenkraemer's party had reached it a few minutes before us, even though they had left Chamonix a quarter of an hour later. It consisted of seven members, the oldest of whom was not five-and-twenty.[2] Mine, still at full strength, consisted of fourteen, including the mule-driver, Auguste Payot, who was accompanying us as porter as far as the Grands Mulets.[3] Some of us were seated, some lying down, some standing, and some perched on the broken stones that surround the main rock itself.[4] Everyone was chattering, eating, and drinking at will. Even the animals were hungry; the pigeon puffed up its crop as big as an egg, and drank accordingly. As for Diane, M. Eisenkraemer's dog, she made short work not only of all her master provided, but of the mutton-bone as well.

Suddenly, we caught sight of the third party. We surveyed each other; its progress was not as rapid as ours had been, for it was advancing quite slowly, and seemed to have adopted the motto: '*Che va piano, va sano.*'

It reached us at last, just as we were preparing to move on. The Polish gentleman came forward to pay his respects with some civil words about being fellow-travellers. Then, seeing that this latest caravan was engaged on unpacking their provisions, we left them thus usefully occupied. We took with us the ladder, agreeing to send it back by one of the porters when it was no longer needed, and set out once more, with my party leading. A few minutes later, I changed my light shoes for woollen stockings and nailed boots. Before us lay the Bossons glacier.

Chapter XII

THE BOSSONS GLACIER

It is strange how great a variety of forms is to be found in glaciers in general, and the Bossons glacier in particular. Not only do these vast masses change every year in shape and appearance, but in the course of very much shorter lapses of time they undergo considerable alteration. Perhaps a pyramid will crumble away, and a crystal palace arise from the ruins. An abyss will close up, but a chasm, deeper yet, will open up a few steps away. It is therefore impossible to know in advance in what state you will find the glacier: whether the ladder will be needed twice or ten times; in short, whether you will be lucky or unlucky. It is a lottery indeed; and the practice is to favour one's chances by sending on ahead two intelligent guides to act as scouts, the first tied on and the second holding the rope. These two men explore the icy wastes, inspecting the route, establishing its safety, ascertaining what is the best point to cross a crevasse, whether an awkward corner will be a short cut, or whether a detour is needed to avoid danger. Such precautions were all the more necessary for us because there had not been an ascent since the 26th of August 1837.[1] The guides were therefore by no means sure of the path they should take; they took turns to lead, accompanied by two porters, and it was a real pleasure, unalloyed by apprehension, to see these men of the mountains in their capacity as scouts. They moved so easily over the ice, they crossed crevasses with so much agility; in short, they seemed so at home on the glacier that I had no thought of peril. When they encountered real obstacles, they would retrace their steps and search for a better way round, after shouting to warn us to stop at this or that point en route.

When they walked on without comment, you could follow in their footsteps, secure in the knowledge that all was safe.

As for the travellers themselves, they must practise greater prudence. In the places where there is danger, they are roped up, for example at crevasses too wide simply to step across without jumping. We encountered some such right from the beginning of the glacier. I submitted with good grace to be tied on, for I had promised; one guide took up a position at the other side of the crevasse and extended a stick, keeping hold of one end; as I leapt forward, he pulled it towards himself, while the other guide let the rope slip through his hands, ready to grasp it should I miss my footing. As you will see, this would prevent, if not a fall, at least the consequences which might ensue were it not for the precautions these good fellows adopt when guiding travellers like myself.

At the outset, I found these precautions much to my taste and abided by them. Half an hour later, I would only accept the help of the stick and rebelled against the rope. Yet another half-hour, and I rejected the stick and advanced by my own exertions, jumping over the crevasses as I saw the guides do. To begin with, they looked concerned; but when they saw the aplomb and confidence of my progess, they said to each other: 'She moves like us and is not afraid of anything! We'll not interfere.'

We were about half-way across the glacier, when our scouts called a halt. They had reached an impassable labyrinth of deep crevasses, ice boulders, and steep declivities. They retraced their steps to a vantage point and looked about for a way through the wilderness. Suddenly, one of them cried: 'I can see the tracks of a chamois!'

If I had not promised my readers to abide by the truth, I would be tempted to tell a little lie at this point: how charming it would be to relate that we sighted a real chamois crossing the glacier, springing across the crevasses with the nimblest grace, and that we followed this novel guide for a quarter of an hour! . . . Alas, I must confine myself to the facts, unromantic though they may be: we did not even see the tip of his horns, only his tracks, pointed out by the leading guide.

At once the guides exclaimed: 'Follow the chamois! Let's follow the chamois! It makes no mistakes, it knows the right way and will lead us safely on.'

So, there we were, treading in the steps of the chamois and trampling with our great hobnailed boots the delicate traces of its little hooves; our whole party looked on it as the angel of the desert.

Suddenly, we heard the scouts' voices: 'An arête between two crevasses!'

'Is it very narrow?'

'Faith, it's only a few inches wide, but if we decide to avoid it, we shall have to retrace our steps and make a great detour.'

'Did the chamois go that way?'

'Yes.'

'Well then, let's follow the chamois,' the guides reiterated.

'And the lady?'

'The lady will go anywhere two men have been before,' I said, with my chin in the air!

'Then we'll follow the chamois,' they chorused.

Behold us then, crossing the arête in Indian file; I, proudly occupying third place as I had stipulated, had no other support than the hand of the guide before me. The rope would have been useless, for it is only of avail if the man holding it can attach himself firmly enough to the ice to resist the shock resulting from a fall. What we needed there was a balancing pole.

A few minutes, and we were off the arête, a path for chamois if ever there was one! A little way further on, since our horned guide had taken the turning for the Montagne de la Côte, we abandoned its tracks and continued our ascent towards the Grands Mulets.

It was almost at the end of this stretch that we first resorted to the ladder; until then, it had been no more than a heavy extra item of baggage for the porters, of no use to us. But we were faced by a crevasse of unusual width and depth. From the ice wall opposite us, there protruded an enormous block of ice; we had no difficulty in fixing our ladder with one end resting on this bastion and the other on one of the sloping surfaces of the crevasse itself. We each went down in turn, balanced on the rock while the ladder was turned round, and then mounted the opposite side. I need hardly add that the ladder, held top and bottom by the guides, was perfectly safe.

We were also glad of it a little further on, at a less difficult spot: a small ice ravine, which we crossed by laying our ladder over it as a bridge. A moment later, we found ourselves in a hollow at the foot of towering cliffs; the beginning of the Grands Mulets rocks, which separate the Bossons and the Tacconaz glaciers. One of our brave band was sent back with the ladder, to leave it where the other members of the expedition would need it; and before embarking on the ascent of the rock face, a short halt was called, during which much praise was lavished on the lady for the courage she had shown so far. The lady in question had always considered such admiration undeserved, since she is by nature adventurous; on this occasion she was more than ever sensible that it was unmerited, since she knew that a much sterner test lay ahead. True, we had so far been blessed with uncommon good luck; the guides assured me that they had never known the glacier *better behaved* (a technical expression).

If I was pleasantly surprised by the difficulties I had anticipated for the crossing of the Bossons glacier, the natural phenomena I had hoped to find there did not come up to expectations. The exquisite needles to be found in the lower regions had promised a whole forest of gigantic ones higher up, and it was accordingly with disappointment mingled with vexation that I would go for a quarter of an hour together without finding a single one of those crystal palaces, those garlanded arcades, or those fairy grottoes which I had thought would delight my every step. However, I did observe some splendid pyramids and several ice masses cast in the strangest forms, and yet I must repeat that these were isolated examples, by no means the impressive array that I had imagined would meet the eye at every turn.

Chapter XIII

THE ROCKS AT THE GRANDS MULETS

The first rock at the Grands Mulets, which we had now reached, is a real fortress which you have to take by assault. It demands a series of gymnastic feats, not without difficulties even for the guides. This is where my mountain upbringing proved its worth. I felt so sure of foot when scaling the rocks that I was even reluctant to be tied on, but my guides wielded the authority with which I had invested them at the bottom of the mountain to cast a rope around my body and to knot it firmly. 'We let you have your way on the glacier,' they said, 'but now things have changed; this is one of the hardest parts of the route, and we cannot allow you to risk your life! Quite apart from the distress it would cause us, it would be a fine thing for our reputation to return without the travellers who set their faith in us, or to bring them back crippled.'

Indeed, they were right; however sure my footing might be on the mountains, it could slip on those vertical rocks. So I abandoned the petty vanity of climbing unroped, and after watching with enjoyment as the rest of the party reached the top, I followed in their footsteps with a confidence and ease that were reminiscent of my prime.

Once at the top of this first rock, the question arose whether we should have to reach our bivouac from the northern side, following the whole line of rocks that make up the Grands Mulets, or whether we could take the southern route which crosses the packed snow at the edge of the Tacconaz glacier. Two guides went ahead to reconnoitre, and once again I was in luck: the snow only yielded a few inches under our weight. We were thus able to avoid an arduous climb over the rocks and to take a route which was longer but easier; in less than an hour we had attained the top of a conical rock of about three hundred feet in height. Seven-eighths of the way up was a little ledge running along the southern side; it was perhaps fifteen feet long by seven wide, protected on the east by a rocky bastion and cut off on the west by a kind of dry wall, six feet high. This was the point at which we were to strike camp for the remainder of the day and part of the night; we reached it at two o'clock exactly, and since my party was too large for such a confined space, we also took possession of another ledge, somewhat smaller, a few feet further down. There we deposited the wood, the provisions, the equipment; in short, anything having to do with cooking.

In keeping with their laudable custom of attending to the wants of their mistress before their own, the guides began by arranging everything for my pleasure and convenience. The blanket seat was reassembled, and above it they erected a shelter using my plaid and four sticks, to preserve me from the burning rays of a hot sun. My Mont-Blanc costume was draped over the rocks, my effects set out to hand, and the jar of lemonade put beside me. Tronchet sharpened my pencils, Desplan fanned me with my great fan, Couttet hung up the thermometer. In short, each took care to attend to my wants before turning his attention to the all-important question of dinner.

After a quarter of an hour's rest, I decided to take my pulse: it was seventy a minute (two less than at the Pierre de l'Echelle), but beating in irregular bursts, which might have threatened the onset of fever, had I not felt in the best of health, both physically and mentally. I examined the thermometer: in the hothouse conditions where I was sitting, I read twenty-four degrees, but when I had it placed in the northern aspect, it dropped to four and a half degrees above zero. Thus, fifteen paces accounted for a difference of nineteen and a half degrees.

The second party soon appeared, and made its camp not far from me, in the hollow between the main part of the rock and the bastion I referred to above.

The third arrived at half-past two, scrambled up in its turn, and settled in about fifty or sixty feet below us. They were also on a ledge, on the western side, but it was very narrow, with a dip in the rock where the Polish gentleman could curl up in reasonable comfort.

Half an hour after the last party had arrived, a communal meal took place. I cannot describe the pleasure I was afforded by surveying from my airy throne this hostelry at the Grands Mulets: at every level it was adorned with groups of mountaineers clustered around legs of mutton, roast chickens, and bottles of wine. There was a general air of self-congratulation that the half-way point had been attained without mishap. Everyone was cheerful, revelling in chatter and a hearty appetite. Nor was the pigeon overlooked; he, too, ate till he almost burst and drank his fill; after which the gleam in his eye suggested he was much refreshed.

As for me, I could not touch a morsel; the light meal I had taken at the Pierre de l'Echelle, my pencils and my thoughts proved ample nourishment till evening.

Dinner over, we took leave of four of our porters and the mule-driver, enjoining them to take with them news of our safe arrival at the Grands Mulets. This they promised to do, and kept their word, as we shall see later. As for Simond and Mugnier, the guides thought it better to retain them; a happy inspiration indeed, for these two good fellows were to prove their worth during the rigours of the next day's journey.

Barely five minutes had elapsed after dinner, when I saw M. Eisenkraemer take out his nightcap, put it on, wrap himself in a blanket and fall into a deep sleep under a little arch in the rock. His faithful Diane lay down at his feet and followed his example. Each guide sought out a comfortable place to rest, and a period of deep silence ensued, very different from the clink of bottles and glasses. Only then could I compose myself sufficiently to wonder at the natural splendours surrounding me, to take up my pencil and preserve them for posterity in the forms of notes and sketches. I shall have more to say later of the three distinct panoramas that make up the view from the Grands Mulets, and of their appearance at the time when their individual features and general effect were seen to best advantage.

At Couttet's dictation, I was busy setting down the names of all the mountains visible in the great bowl on the French side, when the head guide of my Polish fellow-traveller brought me a note bearing the latter's name; he sought permission to pay me a visit in my camp. As you may imagine, I readily agreed; this distraction was all the more welcome since my eyes were beginning to smart and to grow tired, as a result of the dazzle of the snow and also of the notes and sketches on which I had been engaged. The note informed me that my colleague was called Karol Stoppen, and that he lived in Radon, not far from Warsaw. I assumed that he was in exile, but he assured me that he was travelling on a passport from Poland. As you may guess, this country formed the subject of a long conversation, for it was of a consuming interest, not only to the traveller himself, who had much to relate of his homeland, but also to the foreign listener.

After an hour, M. Stoppen took his leave and withdrew. I continued with my notes, and the guides, restored by their little rest, discussed the morrow's departure; they decided that two o'clock in the morning was the most favourable hour, for then the snow would bear, and we should have sufficient time to reach the higher regions before it became soft. They also decided that two men would set out that very evening to reconnoitre conditions on the route we were to follow later in the night; they would make a path and verify the solidity of the snow-bridges, and, in short, prepare the way for all three parties.

Then we chose David Couttet, M. Stoppen's head guide, and Jean Mugnier, one of our porters, to make the agreed reconnaissance. These two cragsmen took their climbing staffs and a rope, and leapt down our steep rock like so many chamois, and, in full view of all three parties, performed a brilliant first ascent. It was delightful to see with what rapidity they climbed, stamping as they walked to leave tracks in the snow; so accustomed were they to such exertions that they did not even stop to draw breath, as they laid a trail for us to follow across the desolate wastes where we, too, were soon to venture. We watched till at last they disappeared from sight, and yet my eyes remained fixed on the stretch they had last crossed, enthralled as I was by the landscape, austere till then, but now suffused with the glory of the setting sun. Its last rays gilded the brow of the Dôme du Goûter, although its lower slopes, rising above the Tacconaz glacier, were already in shadow. My eyes turned to this glacier, far below, where the crevasses that crisscrossed it were of the same shade of blue as the sky. On the left towered the third rock of the Grands Mulets, bathed in glorious light! The whole scene was imbued with a savage and sublime beauty.

We were beginning to feel some concern at the non-arrival of our two scouts, when we heard the piercing cry commonly adopted in the mountains, and all eyes turned to the point of origin. There was nothing to be seen. Another cry; another vain survey. At last we caught sight of them; somehow, they had reached the very top of the last of the Grands Mulets rocks, and were perched on that vast pillar like pygmies. We signalled to them, and when they were sure we had seen them, they disappeared. The guides seemed anxious at their mode of descent, but were quickly reassured, for the two brave fellows soon reappeared on the snow and returned to their respective camps three hours after they had left the Grands Mulets. They raised our hopes for the next day's climb, for they had found the bridges firm and the snow in good condition.

They told us why they had ventured on the rock where we saw them, and Mugnier confessed that he was responsible, having persuaded his companion to go geologizing. They produced some fine specimens of epidote and tourmaline which they presented to me. Couttet had also been prospecting on our own rock, and had given me some asbestos and a stone with little pyrites embedded in it; I treasure all these keepsakes, along with the only two plants I could find at the Grands Mulets: one, of the species *graminaceae*, is called poalaxa, the other a *Saxifraga bryoïdes* of the least conspicuous variety.

Having thus accounted for the mineral and vegetable kingdoms, we must not neglect the animal. Since we had stopped, we had seen no other living creature, till all at once I caught sight of something running a few steps away from me: a white mouse. How was such a thing to be believed, there, on this solitary rock, in the middle of the eternal snows? How had it come to be there? How long ago? What did it live on? . . . I cannot tell. But I saw it; and seeing is believing. A mouse! 'Five francs for it, alive or dead!' I exclaimed. The poor creature was immediately assailed by a hail of stones, but had the good fortune to escape, and vanished into a crack in the rock. Although I would have liked its skin, I kindly scattered a bountiful supply of crumbs, all that remained of our meal, in front of the hole where it was hiding – a larder of goodies for three months at least!

Night was falling, the thermometer only read ten degrees above zero; I had resorted, in turn, to my boa, my plaid, and my cloak, only to find that even these were of little avail at ten thousand feet.[1] I contemplated changing into the costume I intended for the glorious summit; but was greatly perplexed how to achieve such a toilet, exposed as I was to sky, earth, and above all to three-and-twenty male observers. I asked the guides to assist me; in no time they had fashioned a sort of cubicle from a suspended sheet, where it was quite in order for me to divest myself of my dress and to put on my thick trousers, my boots, and my blouse. That was not all; one of the bodices laced at the back, and I needed assistance. I asked for the most adept; Desplan was deputed, by general consent, but he had gone to the northern part of the rock to collect snow for melting. Favret appeared as substitute, and acquitted himself so skilfully in his novel capacity as lady's maid that I could not have been better waited upon, had Jeannette herself been there.

The conversation turned to supper, and this time the guides decided to regale themselves with a kind of hot beverage peculiar to them, which they call lemonade, but which seemed to bear a close resemblance to 'Mother Gibou's tea',[2] seeing the great variety of ingredients of which it was composed: melted snow, brandy, vinegar, sugar, lemons, and even, I think, a little salt. It was all tipped into the saucepan at random; Couttet assured me that it was the best drink in the world, but I preferred to take it on trust rather than risk such a dubious concoction.

I asked for supper; this time, helped by a healthy appetite, I disposed of a spread that would not have disgraced a schoolboy. However, it was the only meal I really enjoyed throughout the whole three-day expedition.

Chapter XIV

THE CONCERT AT THE GRANDS MULETS

When supper was over, we set about erecting the tents; mine was elegantly embellished with two candles impaled on sticks, against the brief darkling[1] that preceded the rising of the moon. Before our time of rest, I was eager to enjoy some of the mountain songs of the region, among others 'Evening Hymn', much praised by several of my predecessors. I supposed it to be a religious song, of an elevated character much in keeping with the wild majesty of the surroundings. I begged Desplan, whom I knew to be the singer of the party, to perform it; but he had never heard of it, and relayed my request to M. Stoppen's camp, where there were all the Rubinis of Chamonix.*

'The "Evening Hymn"! . . . What's that, then – do you know?' was the general enquiry.

'No. Ah, but wait; perhaps it's this one:

> Every night, my divine,
> I think of good wine
> And when I do
> I drink to you!'

'No, no, my friends, that's not it; I wanted the "Evening Hymn" and not a drinking song.'

'The "Evening Hymn"! It must be this one, then:

* *Translator's Note*: Rubini, Giovanni (1794–1854). Great Italian tenor who enjoyed sensational success in Paris, London and St Petersburg. He had an enormous range and the tenor roles in *Il Pirata, La Sommnabula, I Puritani* and Donizetti's *Anna Bolena* were composed for him.

Tonight, sweet Isabelle,
I sail the ocean swell,
And my sailors true
Will fight for you.'

'No, no, you mistake me; it can't be that one either.'

'Well, what can it be then, this "Evening Hymn" of yours?'

'I am sure it is a religious song;[2] you sang it last year, here at the Grands Mulets;[3] oh, do try to remember!'

'Ah, I wasn't there,' said one.

'Nor was I, nor I,' said the others.

'In that case, sing whatever you choose.'

And with that, the concert at the Grands Mulets was under way. I have already remarked that the singers were almost all in M. Stoppen's camp, and they were the moving force. Seated in a circle round the hearth, they lustily struck up the local songs, and Mont Blanc resounded with their cheerful music. They were soon joined by Desplan and one of M. Stoppen's companions; and nobody who heard the joyful serenade that rose from our firelit camp would have suspected that in a few short hours the same men would encounter every kind of danger and, perhaps, death itself!

I was reminded of such thoughts by the threatening sound of an avalanche coming down from Mont Maudit with a thunderous roar! . . . What a cacophony!! The singing continued unabated, but the contrast between the two inspired thoughts of a very different nature in me. In my heart I renewed the prayer I had made when we left Chamonix, and God is my witness that I prayed more fervently for the safe passage of my companions than for the success I longed for on my own behalf.

As a closing item, they rounded off the concert with a shepherd's song, and then a song in the Chamonix dialect. Since they assured me it dated back for centuries and was well-known in local tradition,[4] I append it here as an example of the mountain patois.

Chamonix patois	*Translation*
Lous Prinssos fàn bin lé tailles	The princes set the taxes well
Commet pû ton leu aidi	How can we help them?
I invantant bin des canailles	They make many villains
Qui fan mai qu'on ne leu dit	Who do more than they are told.
I invantant tant de ghens	They make so many people
Per archi et pé sarghens	Into archers and sergeants
I ruinant bin dés ménajho	They ruin many households
Chantins à nutro lengajho	Let us sing in our own language.
Nos, qu'en tata la penna	We who have all the trouble
De labara tu lou blaz	Of ploughing all the corn
Mos mijhin lou pan d'avenna	We eat oaten bread
Et unco vûlant e nos troblaz	And still they want to oppress us.
Parmi nûtra pauvreta	In our poverty
Ino j'ifaut tôt chuportâ	We must suffer everything.
No qu'en tot le demmaijho	We who have all the trouble
Chantins ar nôtro lengajho	Let us sing in our own language.
Nos qu' allins à la trâbla	We who go to table
Avue lou cutais in la man	With a knife in our hand
Nôs copins lou pan d'avenna	We cut oaten bread
Et leu copant le pan blanc	And they cut white bread.
Avue de tartisses et de laitia	With potatoes and milk
Et un bacon de motta mollia	And a little white cheese
Quâqui pou de consenajho	A few vegetables.
Chantins à nûtro langajho	Let us sing in our own language.
Quand i vindra la fin du mondo	When the end of the world comes
Commet e qui faran tu	What will they all do?
I vudrions bin etre d'en nombro	They would like to be numbered
De celeux qu'en bin vécu	With those who have lived well.
Mais quand i sarant jhudia	But when they are judged
I sarant bin motia	They will be caught indeed
I vudriant rendre lou dommajho	And they would like to make good the harm they did
Chantins à nûtro lengajho	Let us sing in our own language.
Fin	The end

Chapter XV

THE BIVOUAC

The singing ceased; everyone's thoughts turned to repose, and the necessary preparations were made. But how could I have followed my guides' suggestion that I should retire to my tent at the very moment when the moon's earliest rays were illuminating a scene, which had certainly been beautiful in the glorious sun of the third of September, but which now attained new heights of poetic enchantment?

The various peaks of Mont Blanc were silhouetted black against the great mass of the Brévent, whose summit gleamed in the first moonbeams; the rounded humps of Pourmenaz, and of Villy, the des Fiz rocks and the jagged peaks of Salanton, still in shadow, contrasted with the snowy summit of the Buet, which rose, brilliantly illuminated in all its grandeur, from the turreted massif around it. Framed by the Buet and the des Fiz rocks, a diversity of mountains could be seen, mistily indistinct at first; but gradually their individual summits cleared, stood out from each other, and could be identified: Sixt, Mounts Agrédon, d'Abondance, les Voirons, Salève, culminating in the Jura range.

I was intoxicated by the spectacle before me; I longed to spend the whole night contemplating it! But, as always, the prosaic side of life impinged on its delights: the guides, who could not sympathize with my ecstasies of admiration at the mountains they knew so well, urged once more that the party should retire for the night without more ado. Unfortunately, they could not do so independently of me, because of the relative positions of our so-called beds.[1] And so there was nothing for it but to stretch myself on the unyielding rock, and to allow the gorgeous scene to be hidden from me by the coarse, brown canvas of my tent.

A quarter of an hour after everyone had settled, twenty-three people were slumbering peacefully on the Grands Mulets rocks. Only one tossed and turned, sat up, lay down, pulled the blankets over her frozen feet, rubbed her stiff neck and battered body: in a word, suffered all the mortification of physical discomfort without the allaying satisfaction of intellectual enjoyment. 'Ah! How hateful a lodging I have here at the Grands Mulets!' she exclaimed at last, after more than two hours' suffering; but this was the voice of one crying in the wilderness, and fell on deaf ears.

Since sleep eluded me, I made amends with a different pleasure: I arranged an aperture in the tent by pinning up a corner of the canvas. Peering out of this little window, I was able once again, to my indescribable delight, to feast my eyes on the scene I had so admired before. Now, the light had changed, giving rise to new effects; and indeed a whole new panorama had opened up to the south-west. In the foreground was the Tacconaz glacier, whose glittering masses contrasted with the black rock of the same name, now completely shadowed. Behind, the Col de Voza, the Prarion, and the Forclaz above Saint-Gervais; on the right, the splendid Aiguille de Varan; these four mountains were also in shadow, but their peaks were haloed with a luminous glow. Below lay the Sallanches valley with the gleam of the River Arve, above which the Dorons and Aravis ranges rose from encircling wisps of cloud.

The moon, three-quarters full, sailed calmly across a sky studded with stars: not a breath of wind! not a whisper in all this wilderness! Nothing spoke of the earth as we know it. I felt I had been transported into a new world, that the great mystery of creation would be revealed to me on this mountainside, and that my proximity to the heavens would expose me to divine inspiration.

What, I wondered, are these planets, these stars that shine so brightly above my head? Are they the abode of creatures destined, like us, for joys intermingled with sorrows, that will culminate only in death? Or does their life run a course more enviable than our own? Were their souls always incarcerated in a fleshly prison, or were they free from bodily constraints, created from birth to know and comprehend some part of the mysteries that surround us?

Such celestial contemplations led me to consider the more exalted questions with which the human mind is preoccupied; I presumed to touch on them all and to amplify some. But vainly do we attempt to peep behind the veil that obscures the future! No ray of light can illumine that impenetrable darkness! And yet it seemed to me that a voice spoke to me from the sky, and said: *Do what is right, and follow your path with confidence.*

An immense avalanche distracted me from the surging exhilaration of such thoughts. You cannot conceive the impression made by this mighty voice of nature, in the midst of solitude! It inspires fear tinged with awe. And when the possibility of peril for oneself is linked to the realization that others too are threatened, the only relief is to be found in fervent intercession: 'Preserve them, oh God, from the dangers to which I am exposing them!' Which is what I said every time this novel form of thunder was to be heard.[2]

Abandoning such supernal preoccupations, I shifted my gaze to what was happening around me. Turning round, I fashioned another window at the end of my tent, and, craning out from it, I saw, in brilliant moonlight, the three camps fast asleep on our rock,[3] with here and there lone sleepers dotted about, who had failed to find a niche in their camp proper and had sallied forth to billet where they could. I saw one, believe it or not, stretched out on the very edge of a rocky projection two hundred feet above the glacier, with his legs dangling over the chasm below! I thought I could make him out to be Jean Mugnier and indeed I was not mistaken. He was sleeping there for all the world as if he were at home in his mill at Frasserend; this was the rest he needed between the twofold exertions of the previous day and the strain of the day to come, when he would walk for eight hours continuously at the head of our three ascents. Since he belonged to my camp, I was tempted to call to him and urge him to choose a safer spot, but I feared that such an action might have a similar effect to awakening a sleepwalker in the midst of great danger, and so dared not disturb this heedless cragsman as he slept on in what for ordinary mortals would be terrible danger!

At last it was time to rise. The first awake roused the others, the ant-heap stirred, repose was succeeded by activity, silence by sounds; and at the Grands Mulets all was the bustle of departure. Some delayed breakfast till we should halt at the Grand Plateau, while others devoured there and then what victuals they could, with a glass of wine. As for me, I ate twelve cooked prunes that remained from the previous day, and drank a cup of soup. Such was the meagre breakfast that sustained me up to the summit and down again to the Grands Mulets.

I much desired to be ahead of the other two parties, in order to claim the glory of being first to set foot on the summit, but Couttet advised me sagely that it would be better to cede that particular honour to our fellow travellers and reserve for ourselves the advantage of following in their tracks. He pointed out that, for a lady, the very ascent was an act of courage in itself, and did not need the added lustre of unnecessary travail en route. He had reason on his side; I yielded and agreed to be the last to leave the Grands Mulets.

Chapter XVI

OUR DEPARTURE FROM THE GRANDS MULETS

It was two o'clock when the first party set off, which was M. Eisenkraener's; M. Stoppen and company followed soon after, and I brought up the rear, accompanied by my six guides and the porter, Simond. We had parted with Mugnier so that he could help lay a track for us: he walked in front, leading tirelessly throughout the three ascents and making a trail for us with that same courage that he evinced from the outset.

The parties were somewhat apart, but still within sight of each other, and as we climbed we could all see our twenty-three companions as we forged ahead along the track to the Dôme du Goûter made the previous evening. The three foreigners could be distinguished by the sticks held for them by two guides, fore and aft, which supported them like a banister. I took advantage of this assistance, although only where necessary, and found it so convenient that I declared myself astonished that the ascent of Mont Blanc should be so simple. 'You'll change your tune on the way down,' they replied; and indeed, this part was very much plain sailing: the track was clear, every footstep was obvious, the snow bore wonderfully well, the long rest had revived us after the fatigues of the previous day, the cold was most moderate, and the weather promised splendidly. Never was seen such eagerness on a journey: I felt light as a feather, anxious to press on fast. 'Slowly,' said the guides, 'slowly! Walk as if you did not want to reach the top.' And their steady, measured advance forced me to keep pace, imprisoned as I was between the two sticks.

After the Grands Mulets, the crevasses become quite different from those on the glacier: instead of the narrow fissures found there, they are chasms, seemingly bottomless, and perhaps fifteen, twenty, or even twenty-five feet wide. They are crossed by means of natural ice bridges;[1] and when the party reaches one of these danger-points, a halt is called. One guide is roped on, and crosses the bridge alone, probing the snowy surface with his stick and putting all his weight in the middle of the bridge so as to test its safety. When he reaches the other side, a second follows, then a third, and so on until the whole party is over. The reader will understand the importance of never risking more than one at a time on these delicate bridges; although they may be strong enough to bear the weight of a single person, they would crumble if more ventured on together, and then what a terrible disaster would ensue! For the inevitable consequence of a fall into such an abyss would be death.

For the first hour of walking, I only performed these perilous crossings with extreme caution, as quickly and as lightly as I could and with the thought of danger forever in my mind. But familiarity soon bred contempt, and by the end, I was treading the bridges as nonchalantly as any drawing-room floor, without concerning myself in the least about the precipices that they concealed.

We reached the Petit Plateau at a quarter to four and continued on our way without stopping. As we climbed, the cold became more intense; it aggravated the stinging in my eyes and burnt my face, even though I had taken the wise precaution of rubbing it with cucumber pomade before leaving the Grands Mulets. I attempted a further provision by adding my velvet mask, but could not tolerate it for more than five minutes, as my breath, trapped between mask and skin, worked on me like scalding steam. I resorted to another method: I lowered the green veil attached to my plaid bonnet and fastened it round my neck, but experienced the same discomfort as before, though to a lesser extent, it is true. There was another drawback: a gentle breeze was blowing which fluttered the double layer of gauze over my face and gave me vertigo, and so I was soon forced to tuck the veil back under my bonnet. Moreover, the dazzling snows proved fatiguing to eyes already affected. I reproached myself for having omitted green spectacles from my Mont-Blanc impedimenta, and Desplan offered me his; but since the brilliance of the snows still blinded me to either side of the spectacles, I found the alternation of green and white light strained the eyes yet more. Needs must brave the threefold effects of cold, wind, and refraction with face and eyes quite unprotected.

Between the Petit and the Grand Plateau, there is a passage where a particular danger threatens. You skirt the Dôme du Goûter, which is here surmounted by a ring of séracs;[2] its steep slope is riven with deep cracks that might be avalanches, poised to overwhelm the traveller at any minute, and towering over immense gaping crevasses.

At this point, the guides called for speed and silence, and the members of the party split up to make their separate ways at some distance one from another, thus avoiding the vibration that might ensue from a mass advance or an unwary shout.[3] In this way, if hard fate decrees that an avalanche or sérac should fall just as a climber passes by, the gap between us reduces the likelihood that more than one will perish. Such moments of danger are invested with a certain solemnity: the deep and universal silence, the rapid pace; each climber has a hunted air, as one who fears to look back and see the enemy he dreads in hot pursuit.

We reached this notorious spot: the marks of a recent avalanche and the presence of countless séracs scattered over the ice were ample proof that the danger was not imaginary. In the vicinity rose several snow-pyramids. Distracted by the beauty of my surroundings, I forgot the perils, and almost suffered the fate of the astrologer in the story: eyes turned heavenward to admire the overhanging blocks of ice, I felt the ground give way beneath me, one of my legs plunged into the snow, and my foot dangled in mid-air . . . I was standing on one of the little bridges spanning a crevasse which I described above; weakened by the passage of two-and-twenty persons, it had yielded, leaving me marooned above a deep but narrow chasm. 'Help! Help! come quick!,' I cried; the two guides before and behind me ran up, extending helping hands and supporting sticks so that I was soon out of danger. However, I did not escape without a little lecture: 'Instead of gazing at dangers far off, look to those beneath your feet,' said my rescuers. How right they were! and from then on I crossed such abysses with the greatest possible caution.

Chapter XVII

THE GRAND PLATEAU

After crossing the Grand Plateau, we reached our resting-place at a quarter to six; the thermometer read nine degrees below zero. Although this temperature is by no means intolerable, and I rejoice in the cold, I cannot well describe the bitter chill we felt then: it penetrated to the very marrow, and everybody was pale and trembling. I was forced to put on my pelisse, to lower my veil, and to clap my hands together in an effort to achieve some warmth. I do not know what it was in the air of the Grand Plateau that made it so piercing; it remains a fact that I never experienced such cold in my whole life.

We found the two other parties at breakfast, and mine soon followed suit. Some said they stood in great need of nourishment, while others claimed to have no appetite. I was among the latter, and even experienced a certain revulsion at the sight of food, and so I left the guides to apply themselves to chickens and wine, while I explored the surroundings.

The Grand Plateau is an area of smooth snow 11,750 feet above sea level. To the east, it is dominated by the slope leading to the Corridor;[1] to the west, by the Dôme du Goûter; to the south, by the dome of Mont Blanc itself and Les Rognes;[2] to the north, sharp, jagged rocks form an abyss that separates it from the upper part of the Bossons Glacier; and finally, to the north-east can be seen the mountain ranges that I remarked upon at the Grands Mulets and will not describe again. But what struck me as altogether new was the actual position of this enormous bowl, and the view it offered of the pyramidal crevasses of the Dôme: viewed from that quarter, they appeared of gigantic size.

Since we had left the blankets at the Grands Mulets, one of the guides' bags did duty as a seat. I tried, before we continued, to make a few brief notes, but was soon forced to desist by the condition of my fingers, stiff with cold, which permitted no more than a few lines. I also intended to sketch the pyramidal crevasses of the Dôme, but that proved quite impossible; indeed, one of my hands was suffering from a painful numbness which I rubbed briskly with snow. This at once restored circulation; and it was in the best possible condition, both physical and mental, that I left the Grand Plateau and returned to my two sticks. It was then a few minutes past six.

Chapter XVIII

FROM THE GRAND PLATEAU TO THE CORRIDOR

Two ascents were already under way when my turn came to set off. M. Eisenkraemer's party had quickly taken the lead, for they were all young, including the leader: but I soon caught up with M. Stoppen's group and from then on there was only a small gap between us.

I was dauntless on the climb above the Grand Plateau; I felt so well, that I once more declared myself astonished that the ascent of Mont Blanc should be so easy. Although my guides were pleased for me, they were also somewhat scandalized at such an irreverent attitude towards His Majesty, King of the Alps, and in their amazement kept repeating: 'She is not tired at thirteen thousand feet up! A woman! Incredible! Unheard-of!' Even before we reached the Grand Plateau, several had been complaining of exhaustion, and since we had halted it had increased: one was suffering from a migraine headache, another from cramp in the hamstrings, a third from nausea, a fourth from sleepiness . . . in short, everyone, apart from my head guide and Simond, the porter, was suffering to some degree. Almost an hour after we had left the Grand Plateau, I felt a little stiffness in my back, accompanied by heaviness in the eyes. This heaviness soon became an overpowering need for sleep; I told the guides, who advised me to resist it for as long as possible. I struggled on for almost an hour, but was obliged to sit down for one or two minutes, at first at every hundred and fifty paces, then after a hundred and twenty, a hundred, eighty, and finally after sixty paces. On one of these stops, I took my pulse before moving off again: and found it to be a hundred and thirty-six a minute.

I could not struggle any longer against the sleep which was overpowering me: I confessed my need for a moment's rest, which I deemed aggravated by my sleepless night at the Grands Mulets. The guides were not mistaken in their view that this desire for sleep had more to do with the climatic conditions than with the previous night's insommnia. However, they granted me six minutes: one of them sat down on the snow, I was seated back to back with him, so that I was supported in a more comfortable position than with my head in my hands. Two other guides followed suit and propped each other up in a similar way. The remaining four kept watch over the sleepers, and woke us with implacable punctuality at the end of the time allowed. What a cruel awakening for me from pure bliss!

This short rest benefited me greatly, and for a period of almost twenty minutes I was once more able to complete the allotted hundred and fifty steps. But then it dropped by tens to sixty, which had become my standard tally by the time we attained the foot of the ice wall. It was half-past nine. There we found Jean Mugnier, who had been told to wait for us at this point. Not content with the scouting duties he took on at the Grands Mulets, he had accumulated others galore in the shape of a great pack on his back, six inches taller than himself, and topped by the pigeon in its cage. So, my party was back to strength, but how tired we were! In what a state! Pierre-Joseph Simond was in the grip of a violent migraine that had grown steadily worse since the Grands Mulets. Favret was suffering from pains between the shoulders, and from sickness and vomiting, Desplan from palpitations and cramps. Tronchet was hungry, thirsty, sleepy, and suffering spells of compression in the head. Jacques Simond was hamstrung and could hardly continue. Couttet and the two porters were the only ones still fit, although I, too, felt in condition, apart from the need for sleep that I had been struggling against for more than nine hours.

Before proceeding further, the guides prevailed upon me to make my way to the end of the Corridor, to give me, as they put it, a foretaste of the view of the summit. I did so and saw . . . But I anticipate; it was all waiting for me up there!

'To the summit! to the summit!' became my war-cry. But what a massive rampart kept me from my dream! A great wall more than three hundred feet high rose before me, almost vertical! Half-way up I could make out M. Eisenkraemer labouring away with an axe: he was cutting his own steps in the ice. M. Stoppen was much lower down, and I now made my way to the foot of that formidable bastion.

Before starting to climb, I thought it my duty to suggest to those of my guides who were so seriously indisposed that they should stop at this point, and rest until our return. None of the good fellows would agree, however: 'A fine thing it would be,' they said, 'if it became known that a lady went up while we stayed behind to cosset ourselves till she came back. We shall all follow you to the top.' And they kept their word.

Chapter XIX

FROM THE ICE WALL TO THE SUMMIT

A Chinese proberb runs like this: *when you have ten steps to take, nine steps are half-way*, and it is a saying that proved its worth to me on my ascent of Mont Blanc.

The previous day I had conquered the Mimont rocks, traversed the Bossons glacier, and performed several gymnastic feats with ease. I had not long since made my way across abysses over little snow bridges, braved avalanches that had happened the day before, while threatened by others that could break at any moment; I had viewed without alarm menacing séracs looming overhead, and had scaled long and short pitches as well as any of my guides. Now, scarcely fatigued, I had completed nine-tenths of the ascent and could not but think myself nine-tenths successful. But now you will learn how victory almost eluded me at the last moment, and how strange was the enemy I encountered in these altitudes.

We began our climb in the following order: Mugnier led, Couttet was second, I was third, Simond the porter fourth, and then the five other guides, mountain-sick as I have just related. But here were no sticks to act as handrails; the geographical nature of the place obliged us to rely on our courage alone.

I had not scaled twenty steps of our ice staircase when I was forced to call a halt, being in a most extraordinary condition: my heart was beating so strongly that I feared my chest would burst, the muscles of my arms and legs seemed to have lost their resilience and to be plunged into a heavy lethargy, my head was swimming and a leaden sleepiness weighed on my eyes . . . I could not withstand it.

'I must sleep a moment,' I said to Couttet, 'my head is full of vapours.'

'Just another few steps.'

'I cannot!'

I barely had time to turn round and slip into a seated position on one of the steps, where I at once fell asleep. After two minutes, the head guide awoke me. I started to climb once more, but the next moment I was afflicted by the same condition, the same overpowering need to sleep. I forced myself to take another twenty steps, but then sleep once more overtook me and I sank down where I stood, this time so clumsily that I almost tumbled down to the bottom.

'A rope, a rope!' cried Couttet. One was passed to him; he fastened me on firmly, gave the end to Mugnier, who was leading, roused me, and we set off again, secure in the knowledge that I could not fall, so provoking an accident which might prove fatal, not only to me, but also to all who were following me up this near-vertical staircase.

Yet again I was assailed by sleep, yet again I was awoken, yet again I struggled on. The same affliction struck after a few moments, and this time, it was impossible to accomplish the twenty paces I had set myself; it needed all my courage to manage even fifteen or sixteen, for the palpitations became so violent that they were near to suffocating me. When we stopped on this occasion, I heard Couttet bemoaning my ever-increasing need for sleep, which threatened worrying delays. 'It's no good! . . . We're in trouble!' he said. 'Look at her, asleep again. This is the last lady I take up Mont Blanc.' The sixteen steps soon dropped to fourteen, then twelve, then ten, which I maintained, though by an effort of will absolutely incomprehensible to those who have not undergone such sufferings. In my particular struggle, suffering became agony.

From the third step onwards, the palpitations were again suffocating; the desire for sleep increased as the strength needed to combat it ebbed away at a terrifying rate. My arms and legs became ever weaker; a raging thirst that seemed unquenchable caused yet greater misery; my pulse could not be counted; one by one, my physical powers were abandoning me: I heard without hearing and saw without seeing. And yet I retained one sovereign moral quality: my will, alone capable of galvanizing into action my poor impotent body! Perhaps thirty times it succumbed to this slumbrous torture, thirty times it struggled up to reach the appointed goal.

There was one moment when I did believe victory would elude me. I have explained that I needed about two minutes rest at each halt. Once, we tried cutting this time, but to no avail, since I had not been three steps before I collapsed in a state of such prostration that it was feared I might be too weak to stand.

'If I die before reaching the summit, promise me that you will carry my body to the top and leave it there,' I said, my eyes already half-closed.

'Have no fear, you will reach it dead or alive.'

Consoled by this promise, I fell into a deep sleep; I heard Couttet calling my name but I could not move or reply. I was so comfortable there that I felt better able to lift the mountain from the ground than to get to my feet once more.

'Should we carry her?' asked Mugnier. 'I am ready to do so, I am still strong enough. Mademoiselle, do you want to be carried?'

His words released me from my torpor, which melted away, leaving the field free for my will. 'I will not be carried,' I replied. 'I intend to make the whole ascent on my own two feet; truly there would not be much merit in going up Mont Blanc on someone else's back! . . .' Without more ado I picked myself up and continued to climb. The fear of such a humiliation gave me renewed strength, and I outdid myself; but soon after, I had to admit defeat and revert to my regular sleep every ten paces.

Finally, slumber alternating with progress, I at last reached the top of the ice wall. There I found M. Stoppen, who had himself called a halt for a proper rest. And when I expressed myself amazed that he was not considerably further ahead, he explained that he had taken the same measures as I had, though in his case they were occasioned more by precaution than by necessity: he too had rested for a few minutes every ten or twelve steps. He had counted the steps of our ice staircase, and I learnt that we had mounted three hundred and fifty-four. He complimented me on my achievement, for he said that when he had seen my condition, he had abandoned any hope of success as far as I was concerned. He also told me that several times he had been close enough to see my face, and that it had been so convulsed with pain that he was convinced my every halt would be the last, and that I would be forced to turn back.

After a quarter of an hour's rest, and a few minutes' sweet sleep, I felt better, and expressed my desire to continue. I was confided to the two sticks held by the head guide and Pierre Simond. As long as I remained on the level surface that separates the ice wall from the dome of Mont Blanc, all was well; but as soon as the way grew steeper, my former afflictions returned, although with less severity: palpitations, thirst, sleepiness, powerless muscles: in short, the whole regiment! . . . But this time, instead of ten paces, I was able to take twenty or twenty-five without stopping, although I was sometimes asleep on my feet for the last few.

In view of my debilitated condition, the guides had to exert great skill to manipulate the sticks round corners without mishap, for the least instability made me stagger. The same was true of the rope; I was well content to know that I was supported, but it was fatal to try to pull me up, as the only result of any attempts to hasten my progress was that I fell flat on my face in the snow. I had to go gently, conscious that I was sustained by rope and sticks; any other form of active impulsion would only have contributed to my exhaustion by obliging me to adopt a speed that I could no longer maintain.

In this way I gradually drew near my goal. I had fallen into one of my relentless sleeps, when I heard Couttet's voice saying: '*Courage! there is the summit! This time we shall reach it!*' I immediately looked up, and indeed, I could see the summit about thirty or thirty-five paces away from me, in electrifying proximity. Leaping to my feet, I ran rather than walked towards the object of my dreams! . . . I could not have been three paces off, but I could go no further, and sank down, crushed yet again by the inexplicable desire for sleep! . . .

This time, they allowed me five minutes' rest; when I awoke, I untied the rope, now useless, and even rejected the stick, so that it was alone and unaided that I took the three steps that lay between me and victory. At twenty-five past one, I finally set foot on the summit of Mont Blanc and drove the ferrule of my stick into its flank, as a soldier plants his standard on a captured citadel.[1]

Chapter XX

THE SUMMIT

No sooner had I reached the summit, than I underwent a complete revival: refreshing air flowed into my lungs, my sleepiness evaporated, all fatigue vanished, my heartbeat returned to normal, the mists cleared from my brain, and it was in full possession of my faculties that I was able to marvel at the mighty spectacle that lay before me.

And I was indeed standing on the highest point in the Alps, because as far as the eye could see there was nothing above me but a pure sky and the most brilliant sun, while at my feet stretched a limitless panorama! For a moment I stood still, rapt in the contemplation of such majesty, and was preparing to walk round the summit and to note all its details, when my guides urged on me the rest they themselves so sorely needed. I agreed without demur, for having planned from the outset to write a few notes, meticulously headed with the time and place of composition, it was all one to me whether I began with my correspondence or with my walk.

They also reminded me of the pigeon: it was time to release it, so I gave it one last meal, during which I wrote on a card.

'At five-and-twenty minutes past one, Mademoiselle d'Angeville reached the summit of Mont Blanc, accompanied by eight other persons. She would like this pretty messenger to bear the news speedily to Chamonix, and requests M. le Curé to be kind enough to note the hour of its arrival.'

I rolled up the paper and had the cage unfastened. While they were disentangling the willow branches of which it was formed, the prisoner within danced with impatience on its little pink feet; I attached the paper to one of them and tossed the bird up into space. It headed straight for the Dôme, where it dropped down. We thought it must be lost; but a moment later it took off again, crossed the Tacconaz and Bossons glaciers, and disappeared from view. The speed of its flight suggested that it would reach Chamonix in a few minutes, but in vain did we watch for the white flag.[1] The poor bird, less fortunate than the one in the fable, never returned to the dovecote.[2]

The pigeon gone, I set the thermometer on a bundle of sticks: it read eight degrees below zero in the sun. I took my pulse, which had dropped to a hundred and eight beats a minute, seven minutes after I reached the top. I inscribed these few notes in my little book, then, seated on my snowy throne, with my face turned to France and Geneva, I wrote a number of letters to my friends and relations to serve as a constant reminder that I had not forgotten them even on the summit of Mont Blanc. I intended to write two or three more, but my guides implored me to spare them a longer sojourn at an altitude where several of them were experiencing such torment while I felt so well. So I finished my correspondence and embarked on my walk, accompanied only by Couttet and Desplan.

The summit is a sort of elongated hump, perhaps two hundred feet long by thirty wide; widthways, it is nowhere flat enough for three people to stand level with each other. The surface is of hard, flaky snow, half-way between soft snow and ice. I have already recorded the temperature there on the 4th of September at half-past one. I will now turn to the immense panorama which surrounds it.

Whichever way you turn, all you can see is range after range of mountains, but their character varies according to direction, so that the view is constantly changing. It resembles an immense picture-gallery, laid out as a reward for the danger the intrepid explorer had encountered on the way up. Predominant is the perspective to the north-east, because of the grandeur of the entire massif of the high Alps. Anywhere but Mont Blanc, their towering forms would seem to threaten the very sky; here, uniformly grey and girdled by clouds below their myriad peaks, they looked like an ocean, with the summits as waves. At the near end of this gigantic range stands the Jungfrau, and then the guides pointed out the Wetterhorn, the Gemmi, the Saint Gothard, Monte Cervina, and, to the west, Monte Rosa, with its cluster of snowy summits rising majestically above this sea of clouds and mountains like an immense citadel emerging from the bosom of the deep.

To the east, the valleys of Courmayeur and Aosta seemed like precipices, lying at the foot of these great mountains, and I could make out several villages in them. But I quickly averted my eyes from such small, mean objects, surrounded as I was by the sublime heights that told of the presence of the Creator! The only abode I could have deemed worthy the scene was the monastery at the Great Saint Bernard, cradle of so many charitable acts, where holy men devote their lives to caring for humanity. But it was hidden behind a wall of mountains; the guides could only indicate in which direction it lay.

In the east, as in the south-east, a perfect view is similarly impeded: it was not the plains of Lombardy, dotted about with their many cities, that I yearned to see; it was the sea, whose grandeur would have so greatly enhanced the prospect. Vainly did I enquire after it and seek to identify it; I could not deceive myself! And yet the aether was limpid and cloudless, the weather brilliant, and my telescope first-class. I could not suffer this disappointment with resignation and committed, I confess, the sin of envy when I remembered those of my predecessors who had had the good fortune to see what I so vainly sought.

In the south, the eye follows the Mont Blanc massif up the ridges that are linked to the summit by a long arête of small rocks.

To the west, several leagues off, the lake at Annecy and the surrounding countryside are clearly visible. This vista, however, is devoid of special features and much like any other mountain view.

To the north-west, a snowy *arête* ran from our feet to the Dôme du Goûter, and beyond that I recognized the various mountain ranges I had seen from the Grands Mulets; now, however, they were seen in a tumbling perspective that gave them the air of an enormous ladder, with the Jura as the uppermost rung.[3]

Not without the liveliest emotions did I gaze upon this, the distant threshold of my own beloved country. My thoughts transcended this barrier and ranged over space and time, places and events . . .

And in this state of high exaltation, my soul framed an ardent invocation for the glory and good fortune of France.

The naked eye could also discern the part of the lake of Geneva lying between Salève and les Voirons, from which I could deduce the position of Geneva itself. Heart and hand sent a greeting to this town, a second home to me now after many years of residence bringing with them happy memories of friendship.

At the foot of Mont Blanc the Chamonix valley stretched northwards. I could see the town itself, and the thought of the many spy-glasses even then trained upon us gave rise to a little swell of pride at our triumph, gained in full view of a large and distinguished audience. It was mingled with true pleasure at the realization that the earlier anxiety of all our relatives would be dissipated now that they were able to count us and see that the most difficult and dangerous part of the journey had been completed without mishap.

Above Chamonix is another group of mountains, chief among which is the Buet, and, finally, there is the view along the Mont Blanc massif itself, encompassing all its peaks. Anybody who has set foot on these has no trouble in recognizing the various pinnacles, the glaciers, the paths, and the principal view-points. Among other features, I could make out the green sward of le Jardin, set like a little island in the eternal snows. To the right, the Grandes Jorasses, then the Aiguille du Géant, and then the Mont Maudit, standing like an outpost a few hundred feet below us.

This, then, is the prospect from the summit of Mont Blanc, a magnificent view which I had the good fortune to enjoy in brilliant sunshine. The sky arched from deepest blue above to pale blue at the horizon,[4] by a gradation of colour so delicate that it was impossible to distinguish individual hues.

This astonishing sky, the desolation of colossal mountains, the fretwork of clouds and grey peaks, the eternal snows, the solemn silence of the wastes, the absence of any sound, any living being, any vegetation, and above all of a great city that might recall the world of men: all combined to conjure up an image of a new world or to transport the spectator to primitive times. There was a moment when I could believe I was witnessing the birth of creation from the lap of chaos.

'Now that you have seen everything that is visible from the top,' Couttet said, 'You must go higher than Mont Blanc.'

'What!' I replied. 'Is there a path from here to the moon?'

'You shall see.'

He and Desplan interlocked their hands to form a kind of seat, and then invited me to place myself on it, which I did, having some inkling of their intention. The two guides then lifted me from the snow as high as they could, thus in fact elevating me above Mont Blanc to a height which, *pace* masculine pride, was never attained by my predecessors. I am sure the climbing fraternity will not begrudge me this four-foot difference between their achievement and my own, since the credit for its invention does not lie with me.

A summons came for Couttet from the makeshift hospital we had left at the other end of the summit.[5] 'Do make her go,' implored the other four guides. 'The wind is rising, a storm is on its way, and it may be that night will come upon us before we reach the Grands Mulets.' Couttet came back with these tidings; I begged for a little longer but, drawing out his watch, he insisted. It read twenty minutes past two; we had been on the summit for nearly an hour, and those who, unlike me, had not come for pleasure, found that time dragged and their sufferings were hard to bear. I made my way back to them, and as soon as I saw the condition of my poor fellow-climbers, I hesitated no longer. The serious disorders which had afflicted them seemed aggravated. Tronchet, among others, alarmed me: he was purple, his lips were split and bleeding in several places, as well as other parts of his face. Pierre-Joseph Simond's migraine was at its most acute; his cousin, Jacques, was suffering from blurred vision; Favret was deathly pale and ill. Shivering, they all begged for a departure it would have been inhuman to delay. Desplan, although recovered in himself, was purple, and his blackened lips were covered with countless blisters. Couttet was the only one of my guides whose features had remained unaffected; he looked exactly as he had done when he left Chamonix. The two porters were also in fine fettle.[6] I wondered how I myself looked; I drew out my little mirror and was horrified: my face was swollen, also my nose and lips; all the whites of my eyes were reddened and veined with crimson; my skin was burnt by the cold and I was purple from the roots of my hair to the tip of my chin; in short, I was a real monster! Apart from this mask of horror, I was physically and morally in the best of health, and after my rest on the summit I felt ready for another two hours' climb: strong, light of foot and sound in wind and limb.[7]

This, then, was the state of the party when we left the summit. Before taking leave of it for ever, I inscribed my favourite proverb on the snow. '*Vouloir c'est pouvoir*', and then gave the signal for departure. It is with sorrow, nay remorse, that I now recall my ingratitude in leaving without having thanked God for my success. I should have blessed Him on my knees for the splendour of His works that I saw before me; but my imagination was so caught by their poetic side that it engulfed completely the holy thoughts such a scene should have inspired. At other times en route, my conduct was worthier.

Chapter XXI

FROM THE SUMMIT BACK TO THE GRANDS MULETS

Just as we left the summit, the wind, which had strengthened greatly during the hour we spent up there, buffeted my face with a blast of icy spicules; it felt like burning coals and I thought I had been blinded, but I was told it was one of the mountain's favourite little tricks. I promptly turned my back on it. It was suggested that I might like to try the 'glissade' and I readily acquiesced in this mode of descent, as rapid as it is enjoyable. The traveller sits down on the snow, with a guide sitting in front and holding her feet. They are roped for safety, in case they should slither off the path. With a little push, you slide off at speed, and in five minutes you reach the bottom of slopes that before took half an hour to climb. It was in this way that I came down the dome of Mont Blanc.

I had recovered all my earlier strength, so that I almost ran down the part between the highest ridge and the notorious ice wall! Here there was no question of glissading; we would have hurtled down like an avalanche, ending in as many fragments. Indeed, extreme caution was needed on the descent, including reshaping the three hundred and fifty-four steps so that the heel was lower than the toe. The guides went first, and one of them descended immediately in front of me, so that his shoulder was on a level with my hand; thus we came down our ice ladder, slowly and surely, and, for my part, without vertigo (although I was looking straight down into the chasm below us), without sleep, without palpitations, without fatigue. In short, I was completely free from those disorders which had brought me so near to death only a few hours earlier in exactly the same place.

Once at the foot of the wall, we collected the equipment we had left there,[1] and went on our way. Less than an hour after leaving the summit, one of the guides pointed to it and said: 'See, were we wrong to make you leave it?' I turned round, and saw that the upper section of the mountain was lashed by a terrible storm: it was obscured by a fine cloud of whirling snow rising high into the sky, indicating that a furious gale was sweeping the very spot where I had enjoyed such brilliant sunshine! Ah, great God! Only then did it occur to me to honour him. I should have liked to kneel and beg forgiveness for my unthinking negligence! But I was conscious that such an expression of my feelings would have seemed strange indeed in front of so many witnesses. However, in my heart I did thank God most earnestly and gratefully for that peculiar protection.

We traversed the same route as we had in the morning; from time to time we happened across ice debris which had come down in the interim. I strode on like a Miquelet,[2] hardly stopping for rest. Still, a little break of two or three minutes taken at infrequent intervals was certainly beneficial. During one of these halts, my stick slipped from where I had set it down beside me and slithered down a steep slope which led straight to a crevasse. Pierre-Joseph Simond was the first to notice, and drew my attention to it. I sprang to my feet and chased after the fugitive, running like a mad thing, taking great four-foot leaps in my attempt to reach it, and in fact keeping up with it. 'Stop it, stop my stick! I'm losing my lucky stick!' I cried recklessly to the guides, who had already crossed the chasm.

'Stop yourself! Stop yourself!' they called back, 'or you will fall!'

All at once, my talisman vanished into the abyss below, and I was left clinging on to the slippery slope where I had ventured so foolishly, hoping to escape the fate of the stick. My quarry had in fact been fortunate; the rapidity of its fall had given it such momentum that it shot into the opposite wall, where it remained implanted in the snow about thirty feet down. Seeing how sorry I was to lose it, Simond the porter was kind enough to offer to retrieve it. Anselme and Jacques tied him to a rope and lowered him into the crevasse, from which he soon emerged brandishing my stick. As you may well imagine, this incident greatly enhanced its historical interest for me.

The slippery slope I have just described was the last such that we had to cross. After the heat of the day, the snow was softer and less resistant, but I longed to glissade once more; I had acquired quite a taste for this expeditious means of descent. In vain did the guides object that it was becoming difficult; I would not be deterred. In the end they were complaisant enough to agree, but reversed the previous procedure: instead of attaching the group to a rope at the top of the slope, they stood at the bottom and held an end each. Then, launching themselves forwards, they succeeded in propelling the group, in this novel harness, half-way down the slope, amassing great snowdrifts as it went that piled up to either side and behind it.

It was a very different matter from the heady delights of glissading at speed from the summit: a tedious exercise for all of us which had to be abandoned in favour of common or garden walking.

We crossed the Grand Plateau in snow that had already softened considerably; silently we crept past the séracs and, their dangers safely past, we congratulated each other on our escape from the chief perils of the journey. The guides recovered as we lost height, but all complained of an immense fatigue; for my part, I never succumbed to it on the descent, not even on the arduous section after the Grand Plateau.

Until then, we had trodden in the footsteps of our fellow-climbers, and the snow had been little more than ankle deep, but once the Grand Plateau was crossed, we lost their tracks, and made our way as best we could across great expanses of firm snow, into which we sank ever deeper. Finally it came well above our knees, and at every step we had to struggle to lift our foot clear, only to plunge it back into that dreadful morass. It was plain that the snow had suffered much from the inroads of both sun and wind. In this way, however, we descended long and short slopes, crossed all the crevasses without mishap, and finally found ourselves gazing over to our old rock at the Grands Mulets.

'Do you still think it so easy to climb Mont Blanc?' asked the guides, as they floundered around in the snow.

'The ice wall convinced me that there is indeed some glory in its conquest,' I replied, 'but I cannot claim any credit for our present struggles, for I am not in the least fatigued.'

'Ah! Would that we could say as much! It's a dreadful business, going up Mont Blanc!'

'For my part, I'll have no more to do with it,' said Favret.

'Nor I,' said Jacques. 'This was quite enough.'

'The only reason I went up this time,' said Pierre-Joseph, 'cross my heart, was to accompany Mademoiselle, because I was her guide before.'

'I share your feelings,' I returned, 'for once is quite sufficient for a lady to climb Mont Blanc; however, I did observe certain peaks from the summit which I should much like to visit one day.'

Thus engaged in plans for the future, we reached the foot of the Grands Mulets rock, which I confess I scaled with enormous expertise, considering I was but newly returned from the summit. I found M. Stoppen already there, who told me that M. Eisenkraemer and his party had continued down to Chamonix. 'Well done; what splendid fellows!' I exclaimed.

Then, I retired to my bivouac as I had the day before, and found that it was wonderfully well arranged to greet me, thanks to the good offices of Couttet and Mugnier who had hurried on ahead to make all ready for me. It was then twenty-past six; we had thus taken a little less than four hours to cover a distance that had taken eleven and a half on the ascent, a vast difference indeed, accounted for by the ice wall in the morning and the glissade in the evening.

Chapter XXII

FROM THE GRANDS MULETS TO THE PIERRE DE L'ECHELLE

Hardly had I settled on to the little seat that had once more been erected for me at the Grands Mulets, than I was, as it were, rewarded by the sight of one of the most spectacular avalanches on Mont Maudit ever to come down from Mont Blanc (I have this on the authority of Couttet himself). At the very first rumble, I ran for a 'dress circle' position and arrived in time to see the downrush of an immense mass of snow, as it plunged to the bottom of a sort of gully. There it spread out into a great domed sheet and and hurtled on down, with a thunderous roar, into the depths below, where it shot up again to an immense height in a gigantic cloud of snow-crystals.

This splendid avalanche was the first I had ever seen; the night before, I had only heard the noise and had taken it to be an owl's cry! This one happened when all danger was safely past, and delighted my eyes without burdening my spirits with dire presentiments of disaster. It came at the most opportune moment: we cheered, the curtain fell, and the play was done.

Our boots were so much drenched by the long climb down through soft snow that they stuck to our feet and legs and had to be torn rather than pulled off. We made a small fire (for our supplies of wood were running low; and when everyone had warmed themselves at it, our thoughts turned to supper. It was quickly prepared and even more quickly consumed, for most of the guides had lost their appetite through exhaustion, and the prospect of sleep seemed far more alluring than food. We tried to pitch the tents, but it was hopeless: a strong wind had got up and every time we set up one of our flimsy constructions of poles and canvas, it was violently torn down again. We even had to resort to using stones to weigh down the dresses, hats, shawls, and caps that we had left there the previous day, or they would have been whisked away like so many feathers and strewn around all the glaciers of Mont Blanc.

Everyone settled in for the night, and this time, with the full fury of the wind lashing our rock, I longed for the protection of the canvas roof which I had cursed so roundly when it had interrupted my view of a serene sky and virgin prospects. My furnishings had been enhanced by a most welcome addition: M. Eisenkraemer, learning that I had suffered much from cold feet the night before, had left me his fur-lined sleeping-bag. I made full use of this thoughtful loan, and, putting on my pelisse and covering my painful face with my velvet mask, I stretched out on the familiar bed. Everyone wrapped himself tightly in sheets and blankets, and a few moments later all my companions were fast asleep.

As you can imagine, this my stony couch, intolerable on the first night, was no better after the ardours of the day. I closed my eyes as though to summon sleep, but I had apparently exhausted my capacity for slumber on the ice wall, for I did not enjoy one moment's repose! Nor, this time, was there the stupendous view to make amends for my sleeplessness, for it was veiled in cloud, and was moreover very small beer after what I had seen from the summit! I was therefore assailed more relentlessly than ever by the discomforts of the previous night, aggravated by an unendurable burning of face and eyes. In sum, this period of rest was for me a thousand times less tolerable than the moments of greatest exertion, and it was with an indescribable joy that I welcomed the rising sun. Its rays shone on a sight altogether new.

I have told you that the wind impeded the erection of our tents, and that the guides had accordingly swathed themselves in their bedclothes. Their mummified forms, lined up in rows, really gave the impression of a morgue (it was truly chilling!). Then, when they began to stir, extracting head, arms and legs from their wrappings, it seemed a very Resurrection – all that was lacking was the Last Trump!

The words 'time to go' were on all lips, and I was all the readier to comply for the threat of a change in the weather counselled haste. The summit was still obscured: clouds were visible on several other peaks and the air was oppressive.

Before leaving, we decided to finish off the provisions, with the twin purpose of lining stomachs and lightening loads. We breakfasted where we were; I used melted snow to produce the most unpalatable brew of tea in the history of mankind[1] – then, unencumbered by provisions, the party set out at about six o'clock, successfully traversed the rock and the Bossons glacier, and left the ladder at the great boulder which we recognized from an earlier halt.

In this area I collected many specimens of alabaster, quartz, and chlorite. At the end of the glacier I also found a *Ranunculus glacialis* which gave me the idea of pursuing the little Mont Blanc herbal I had inaugurated with the two small plants found at the Grands Mulets. So I collected all the flowers I passed,[2] and have them still as one of the souvenirs of my mountain pilgrimage.

Chapter XXIII

THE RETURN TO CHAMONIX

We had already passed the Pierre-Pointue, when we observed a fire on a little mound nearby, and two people who seemed to be waiting for us, because they were both gazing in our direction. We reached them, and were pleasantly surprised to find a delicious luncheon set out among the Alpine rhododendrons. A bucket of milk, brown bread, fresh butter, honey, cool water, a good fire; and to cap it all, a charming young girl to do the honours of this rural banquet. She and her brother had come to wait for the climbers, and how glad we were to see them there, as we made short work of the inviting repast! I learnt that our pretty hostess was called Sylvie Favret and lived with her family in the chalet at la Para, which is the highest on the slopes of Mont Blanc. I asked for the bill, which I paid, as you may imagine, without demur, and then our party set off once more along with the young couple from la Para.

We soon reached their chalet, for we were walking apace; as for me, I fairly ran through the rocks and bushes almost as though I were still glissading! I was still some way from the bottom, when I saw the guide Dévouassoud approaching with a mule, side-saddled; he said that Lady C***, whose property it was, had instructed him to bring it to me with her compliments, and added that she herself was on her way to meet me with her husband. Since I had bid farewell to many people at Chamonix without knowing who any of them were, I made enquiries about these two and, from what I learnt, supposed them to be the same English couple who had been present at my preparations for departure. Nor was I mistaken; soon after, I saw them coming to meet me, just as Dévouassoud had said. I did not care to ride on the mule; it would only have ambled gently along, while my own legs were wonderfully inclined for walking and would fulfil my wish to reach these kindly strangers as quickly as I might. The latter greeted me with much cordiality, shook hands warmly, and enquired after my health with an interest characteristic of old friends. My Lady presented me with a bouquet of flowers,[1] and both informed me that they had extended their stay at Chamonix in order to see me once more. For a while we walked on together; you may judge what questions they asked, and still more easily the answers I gave, from what you have just read.

At last we reached the Pèlerins wood. Here the mules come into their own once more, for they can walk here without supervision, and I duly found the mule-driver, Payot, and my dear old Moussa waiting ready for me; I remounted and finished my journey as I had begun it.

Two hundred paces further on, I found Jeannette, my maid, whom we had parted from in tears at Chamonix. She was waiting impatiently to welcome me, and the joy this good creature displayed to see me touched me deeply.

Emerging from the Pèlerins wood, I took temporary leave of Sir Thomas C*** and his wife, for they and their guide were taking the path to the Bossons glacier which they had never seen, and an hour later were due to take the coach for Lausanne; but we were sure we should meet again.

A hundred paces more, and I met the mayor of Chamonix, the good M. Simond. He explained that he was determined to be the first from his commune to congratulate me on my successful ascent and to convey to me the lively interest felt for the lady mountaineer by the town in general and himself in particular.

At last I reached the first huts, and at each hamlet or chalet that we passed there was nothing to be seen but people running from their houses with greetings and congratulations for the Lady of Mont Blanc. Some joined our party, and once we reached the main road, various strangers attached themselves to the front, so that on our arrival at Chamonix I found I was surrounded by quite a little procession. As you will learn, I was indeed received like a queen.

For a considerable distance, the road was lined with the inhabitants of the neighbouring villages. In the town itself, the population of Chamonix mingled with large groups of strangers. People had gathered at every window; the belvederes and verandas of the hotels were crowded, and as I approached the bridge, the local boys heralded my return by letting off a fusillade of shots which echoed and re-echoed around the valley.

'Here's to courage, in whatever dress! . . .' 'Hail to the heroine of Mont Blanc. . . !' 'Long live the Queen of the Alps!' Such were the tributes paid to me as I passed. I was much affected to know that I was the object of such universal and lively interest; but this sweet acclaim was soured for me by the absence of any friend or relation to witness it. Wherever I looked, I saw the faces of strangers; the hands that shook mine I had never touched before! Such a reception had much to offer self-esteem, but nothing for true feeling.[2] I realized I owed it to my success, and to nothing more.

'Supposing,' I said to myself, 'supposing an avalanche had swept me away into one of the abysses of Mont Blanc; my courage in facing danger would have been as great, but my welcome would have been very different! Those who now heap praises on me would not have shed a tear, and the general opinion would have been summed up in one declaration: "The foolish woman! Her desire for fame has cost her dear indeed!"'

This thought cast a sudden shadow over the glory of my safe return, and was, above all, an excellent remedy for the tempting pinpricks of pride.

When we reached the hotel, I was set down, and had to push my way through a real throng to mount the steps. There too, there was a great press of strangers and a broadside of congratulations and handshakes. Just as I reached the entrance, a young lady embraced me warmly with the words: 'Dear lady, what an heroic exploit! What a glorious day for womanhood!' Such enthusiasm arose from a real *esprit de corps*.

As for my guides, they seemed both proud and happy at the successful outcome of our expedition, to which they had all made an active contribution. Before taking leave of these worthy companions, I enjoined them to reappear the next day in order to celebrate our happy return with a banquet, at which I myself would preside. I deputed Pierre-Joseph Simond to invite his neighbour, Marie Paradis (the only woman to have reached the top of Mont Blanc before me). I entrusted Couttet with the arrangements for the dinner of welcome; then, having shaken hands with all my noble guides, and thanked them fervently for all their good offices, I retired, to be alone once more in the chamber where, three days before, I had committed to paper what might have been the last farewells to my family and friends.

Chapter XXIV

CHAMONIX DURING THE ASCENT

Less than half an hour after I had arrived, the rain began to fall.[1] No need to describe my relief at being safe from its assaults! I was removing my heavy costume when the arrival of several strangers was announced; they were about to leave Chamonix and demanded admission. I barely had time to fling my pelisse over my shoulders before I was receiving their congratulations; other visitors came hard on their heels, and so it continued for several hours.

However, it was with true pleasure that I greeted Sir Thomas and Lady C*** on their return from the glacier. They desired to take with them a sample of my writing, left me their address, and assured me of their constant remembrances with so much openness and condescension that their departure seemed the loss of real friends.

I was eager to learn just what had been happening at Chamonix during my absence, and when the visitors had finally left, I questioned Jeannette, and this is what she told me:[2]

From dawn onwards, there was already a great crowd of the curious who followed our progress from the Brévent and the Flégère through spyglasses; they saw the three parties meet at the Pierre de l'Echelle and watched part of the crossing of the Bossons glacier. When the porters returned in the evening, they were immediately surrounded and interrogated, and so it became known that we had completed the first part of the journey without incident.

The next day, at early dawn, numerous parties left for the Brévent; every glass was trained on Mont Blanc; they bristled at every window, every veranda, every belvedere, from the main square in Chamonix and from the very fields! They were all fixed on the points we were presumed to have reached by then, where the human eye could only perceive a fine white carpet devoid of climbers.

A lad of fourteen was the first to catch sight of us. Blessed with the hawk-like vision characteristic of mountain-dwellers, he saw with the naked eye what had escaped the notice of all those relying on first-class telescopes.

'Mother,' he cried, 'I can see them under the Dôme, near the Grand Plateau.'

'It can't be them, not yet!'

'But it is, I can make out the three parties.'

And, peering where he pointed, his mother did see the column of our four-and-twenty little black dots as we made our way across the snow. The news spread fast; the spyglasses were trained on a point higher up the mountain, and once our three parties had been spotted in the vast desolation, they were tracked until the last one disappeared from view.

Then the anxieties of the previous days returned more acutely than ever; it was realized that we had reached the danger-point of our expedition, surrounded as we were by séracs, avalanches, and perils of every kind! I mentioned before that one-and-twenty families were concerned for the happy outcome of our ascent: the mothers, wives, and children of the guides poured into church to pray fervently for our safety. Some had even asked that masses should be said for us,[3] and thus the priest at the altar joined these good people as, in the simplicity of their hearts, they implored God to watch over the poor travellers in their hour of peril.

Some hours passed before we should once more become visible. When it was reckoned that the climbers should have reached this point,[4] the spyglasses came out again. It was already half an hour later than the estimated time, and there was no sign of us.[5] General consternation! 'What can have happened to them? What's going on?'

'There they are!' exclaimed several persons at once, and indeed the first party could be observed scaling the slope before the summit. Then there was a pretty long interval between this first group and the two others; but at last the second and then the third appeared, and the spectators were entertained by the novel phenomenon of three simultaneous ascents taking place on the immense amphitheatre before them, culminating in three successive conquests.[6] The tiny figures were counted, and as it was known that the French lady had eight guides or porters, the Pole seven, and the German six, the observers could identify the groups by the numbers; at such a distance, the costume would have told them nothing.

If the visitors were regaled by the sight of this triple ascent, imagine the rejoicing among the good people of Chamonix when they saw that their families and friends had escaped the dangers they had so dreaded! Of course, such dangers still threatened on the descent, since it followed the same route, but then there was such a difference in the speed of progress on the way down! A mishap was scarcely probable. And hope, like fear, is by no means to be controlled by the will. The first part of the expedition had aroused all their fears, the second filled them with confidence, and when the four-and-twenty travellers reappeared at the end of the Grand Plateau on their way down, the head-count was a pure formality; in reality everyone was convinced that all three parties were complete.

At one point, it was believed that the travellers would return that very evening: the tempest on the summit and the presence of certain clouds boded a change in the weather and it was supposed that the climbers would hasten for shelter. It was M. Eisenkraemer who informed Chamonix that his companions would not arrive till the next day.

On the third day, the curious were able to follow every move we made; we were seen to cross the Bossons glacier and stop for Sylvie Favret's luncheon. It was also observed that heavy rain-clouds were descending in our wake and seemed to keep pace with us.

The previous chapter furnished the details of our triumphant return, which united all those concerned in my great three-day expedition, three days which my friends like to refer to jokingly as *The Great Days of my Glory!*

Following these events, I indulged myself in the pleasure of a bath, and when I emerged from it, I felt so well, that I was almost inclined to embark on another ascent! My feet were not at all swollen by the long climb, because I had no trouble in putting on the pumps I had been wearing the day before we set out. No trace of fatigue, and a voracious appetite! In short, were it not for the state of my face, which was afflicted by a powerful burning sensation, and of my eyes, which were seeing double,[7] I would have been in the best of health. I heard the dinner-gong, and since I felt perfectly fit, I returned to my usual seat at the communal table, where, as you may guess, I was subjected to a never-ending stream of questions.

Night was falling, and it was time to withdraw, especially for one who had scaled Mont Blanc. I cast longing glances at the simple couch provided by the inn; in comparison with the rocky pallet at the Grands Mulets, it seemed a bed fit for a king! Gratefully I lay down, and rested quietly through the night till in the morning sleep came, to beckon me through the ivory gates of dreamland.

PART THREE

After the Ascent

Chapter XXV

MARIE PARADIS

I slept blissfully for a full twelve hours, and had just risen, when the door opened to admit a neat little peasant woman, white-haired and small of stature, who came towards me with open arms, flung them round me, and embraced me on both cheeks. This was Marie Paradis.[1]

'Oh, thank you for having thought of me, Mademoiselle; I was told that you invited me to dine with you today; what an honour, indeed.'[2]

'But what could be more natural, my dear Marie; are we not sisters in Mont Blanc?'

'Oh! Who would think a *real lady* could climb it? When they says to me yestereve that a Lady has come to do the ascent, well, I answers: "Ah, but she won't be going no more than half-way up, that lady; now me, I'm a peasant-woman, and I know the country, and I'm as nimble as a chamois, and look now, what happened to me; well, she won't do it, not her: it's impossible!"'

'If something is feasible, it can never be impossible to the determined mind, my dear Marie, and now you see that I achieved what I set out to do.'

'But I wouldn't believe them at first when they says to me: "Marie, the lady has reached the summit, we've seen her there." But then, when my neighbour Pierre-Joseph came to see me yestereve and says: "The Mont-Blanc lady has told me to invite you to the celebration dinner she is holding tomorrow for those who took her there", well, then I did have to believe him, didn't I? And then this morning I says to myself, I says: "Well, now, I must go straight off to see her, dear lady . . . She won't be *haughty*, not if she asks me to dine, and perhaps it would make her happy to see me a little while earlier."'

'And you guessed right, my dear, I am very pleased to see you, and curious too to know all the details of your ascent now that I have completed my own. Everyone has a different story to tell, so you sit down there, and I will ask you questions, and you tell me the answers just as it happened.'

'Yes, Mademoiselle. Oh! but you won't be afraid I might deceive you, now, will you? I am always truthful, you know.'[3]

'Let us begin at the beginning, and go on from there. How old were you when you made the ascent?'

'Thirty,* I was: would you be wanting to see my papers? I have them here with me.' And with that, she handed me the certificate which proved that she had been to the top of Mont Blanc, on the 14th of July, 1808, at the age of thirty.

'Who gave you the idea of such a trip? What was your intention in making it?'

'Ah! Mademoiselle, I was a poor serving-girl; life was terrible hard and I was poor, too. One day, the guides says to me, "Marie, we're going up Mont Blanc, you're strong, you walk well, you should come with us." And then I replies, "And what business have I up there, then?" "Lord, it's all for your own good: you're poor, you need money; it may be you get to the top, for you're a stout-hearted wench, and then all the world will know that a woman went up. Visitors will want to meet you, and they'll pay good money too, and that'll help you." "Oh yes, that's all well and good," says I, "but I'd never get all the way up, for you tell me it's that dreadful, I surely never could." "Gently now, don't be frighened, we'll help you if you can't manage it alone. We'll carry you if need be. You're a good girl, and we'll look after you, you'll see. Just trust in us." And I says, "Well, all right," and so I went up with them. And that's all about it!'

'And how far did you go by your own exertions before exhaustion set in?'

'Well now, after eight hours I was proper done up, because it's hard going in that nasty old snow. The next day, oh, I was tired when we set off again. And the guides, they said to me

* Some sources put her age at eighteen.

"Courage! Courage! You *will* get to the summit!" And then, when I reached the Grand Plateau, I felt I couldn't go one step further, and I lays meself down right there on the snow, and I says: "Better die here than further on." But "Courage!", they says again, "Courage!", and they sets me on me feet again, but I was so poorly, no strength in me legs at all, and puffing away, I was, like hens when they're over-hot.[4] Well, and they gives me an arm, one each side, and so they pulls me along. I had to stop often enough to vomit (saving your presence, Mademoiselle), but they kept on saying "Courage! Courage!" Well! it's all very well to say "Courage", but if you can't set one foot in front of the other, well, you has to stop, don't you? So down I falls, there by them red rocks, and I says: "I'm a-dying," says I, "just you push me into yon crevasse and you go on as the fancy takes you." And then they says: "You're not giving up, having got this far, you're going to the top, so you are," and one takes one side, and another the other, and they pushes from behind, and they pulls from in front, and sometimes they carries me; and in the end they gets me there. But I cannot tell how, for I could neither see nor hear proper; I couldn't breathe, nor speak. And after, they said I was a sorry sight.'

'Do you remember what you saw once you were up? Can you recollect anything that struck you?'

'Oh, I was too poorly! They laid me out on the snow, for me legs wouldn't hold me. I just remember it was white all around, and black down away below, but that's all.'

'And did you suffer on the descent as you had in the ascent?'

'I don't believe I did! but it's all so long ago now, I can't hardly remember. But I do know I puffed and panted all right!'

'And now, my dear, tell me if the ascent was worth all your sufferings, and achieved its purpose. Did visitors pay well to hear of your exploit?'

'Oh yes, indeed; especially at first, they all wanted to see me, and I did right handsomely out of it. Now, it's not so much, but I still get visitors every year, and they always leave me something, and that's worth a fair bit to me now, because, you know, I only have my little house, and the poor field beside, and now that I'm old and can't work so well, I'd be in a rare pickle without a little bit coming in from them.'

'And where do you live? and with whom?'

'My house is in the hamlet of le Bourgeat, in the parish of les Ouches, and my daughter-in-law lives with me. My boy, you see, he's long wanted to go to Paris, but he knew he couldn't leave me alone to work the field, so he gets married and after a month he says: "Mother, here is my wife who will look after you in my place: for my part, I am going to make my fortune in Paris." And off he goes.'

'And how is your son employed in Paris?'

'He is a messenger.'

'Oh!', I cried, astonished, 'He left his mother and his own country for so little? He is well on the way to earn his keep, but not to lay by a little nest-egg for his old age, so that he can live more comfortably than he does now.'

'What can I say? It's his own idea.'

And, taking the initiative in her turn, Marie asked me if I had felt very unwell? If I had been able to go up all alone? If I was well now? I satisfied her curiosity, and each answer drew the same response, 'Lord, how strong you are!'

Since we had no more questions for each other, I instructed Jeannette to see to it that my sister in Mont Blanc was given luncheon, until it were time for the official dinner. As they went out, I could still hear her repeating: 'Lord, how strong she is!'

In her eyes, I am strong, and no more. She sees neither the motives nor the consequences! As for Marie Paradis, her trip, which I had never understood, was explained by our conversation. It was nothing more than a financial venture; the idea was not her own, and the experience, the outcome, and her recollections can be summed up as follows: *I went up; I puffed and panted; I nearly died; they dragged and carried me along; I arrived; I saw white and black; I came down again. Since then, public curiosity has come up with the small sums I was counting on when I went.*

All this is very down-to-earth, I agree, but at least her account displays both candour and naivety, and in my opinion these qualities are more desirable than the humbug with which many people disguise actions which, like hers, are equally founded on and directed at financial gain, but are far less innocent than an ascent of Mont Blanc.

Chapter XXVI

THE GUIDES' DINNER

Hardly had Marie Paradis left me, when I was informed that one of my guides and his wife had called to see me. A moment later another appeared, and gradually all of them came to visit and to enquire after my health, now that a full day had elapsed. I had never felt better, and no less delighted to see what a good effect a night's sleep had had on my fellow-climbers. They were well, but we united in bemoaning the state of eyes and complexion. I handed out phials of distilled water with spirit of Saturn to cool their burning eyes, and cucumber pomade to soothe their painful faces; and all agreed that the relief afforded by these remedies was almost immediate.

I was also visited by M. Stoppen, who told me that he had been in considerable pain as soon as he returned. Like us, he had been burnt by the mountain air, and had great patches of cracked, red skin on his face. However, M. Eisenkraemer was in the worst case in this respect: his eyes were so painful that he had been obliged to wear green spectacles; he could not make even the tiniest movement with his lips as they were covered with blisters, which had also appeared on nose and cheeks: in a word, like us, only more markedly, he bore the stigmata of Mont Blanc, and yet he said '*I vould not haf missed it for the vorlt!*'

Such, then, was the condition of the three travellers the day after the ascent. I spent the day setting in order my little Mont-Blanc herbal and in receiving calls, and indeed, this was the best way to pass the time, for the rain came down in sheets and any walk would have been a real penance.

Evening came, and with it my guests: the six guides, the two porters, Marie Paradis, David Couttet,[1] and the mayor, M. Simond, who was delighted to be included in the feast. A table for twelve persons had been set up in a private dining-room, and under the napkin of each guide was the emolument he had so richly deserved, along with the usual gratuity.[2] I had already given orders for dinner to be served, when I was informed that some visitors, who had arrived that day and much desired to make my acquaintance, wished to know whether they might enter without impropriety. I assented, and the next moment the room was invaded not by a party of five or six persons, as I had imagined, but by a whole army! A silent army, though, if ever there was one, which stared at me as though I were something quite out of the ordinary! And their silence affected me as well: I could find nothing to say to these strange visitors, and for more than a quarter of an hour together we acted out this queer dumb-show and surveyed each other speechlessly. They tried to serve the dinner, but it was impossible in such a crush! I dared not say: 'Please withdraw!' – I could not have opened a conversation so uncivilly. So we sat there and waited till the dumb crew should see fit to release us, and finally one of them came up and shook my hand in silence, likewise a second, and a third, and then all of them trooped past, like Panurge's sheep, and followed suit. Of what nationality were they? I cannot tell, for not a phrase passed their lips to reveal the identity of these mysterious visitors.

As soon as the last of them had left, the first dish arrived and dinner was served at last. The eleven guests entered and took their seats; I was at one end of the table with Mayor Simond and Couttet to left and right, then the guides, the porters, and, at the opposite end, Marie Paradis. No sooner were we all seated than other visitors asked to be admitted, but these were cheerful and talkative, keen to question the guides and eager to know all the details of the ascent whose happy outcome was the object of our celebration. 'The Union Hotel is better than the one at the Grands Mulets,' was the general opinion among the Mont-Blanc party, including me, and particularly Marie Paradis, who, when she recalled the sufferings of her own ascent, had no doubt that her loyalties lay with the present establishment. As the meal proceeded, it became increasingly clear that the combination of spiritual contentment and white wine was reducing her to a state of settled cheerfulness; so that the visitors amused themselves by questioning her and laughing at her replies. They asked her to tell them more about her ascent and why she had undertaken it, and she explained everything as she had done to me, with the same openness.

'When one is poor,' she said, 'one has to save a little here and a little there, as best one can.'

When she was not being addressed, the dear creature reverted to questioning her neighbours about the deeds and conduct of her sister in Mont Blanc:

'Were she very *lagna*,[3] the lady?' she said in her own dialect, half patois, half French.

'Only on the ice wall.'

'And she had no need of carrying, then?'

'No, she wouldn't have it. Faith, she walked better than you!'

'Oh, Lordy, she's strong, that one. Never would I have believed she could've gone right up to the *sonzon*.[4] Tell us, my duck,' she called from one end of the table to the other, 'where was you bred up then, to be so big and strong?'

(Everybody burst into laughter at the familiarity the white wine had inspired.)

'Why, among the mountains and the fir trees just like you, Marie,' I replied.

(Filling her glass) 'To your very good health, my duck, and may you keep strong and live to a great age. (Refilling it) To the health of the Lord Mayor of Chamonix. (Filling it yet again) And now I'll drink again to the health of each one of the lady's guides . . .'

David Couttet began to be alarmed: 'Careful now, Marie, don't drink more than you can take, or you'll make yourself ill.'

'Now just you leave me be, an' you'll see. (She rose to her feet, made her way to the other end of the table and raised her glass to the guide nearest me:) There, now, you first. (Toasting him, drinking and then moving on to the next, who was Pierre-Joseph:) Now you, next along. (Raising her glass and drinking again; and so on until she had gone right round the table; the same glass doing duty for the nine guests, guides and porters:) Now you see, you great silly, I came out of that right well; did you think I would get the worse for liquor?' she asked David Couttet, as soon as she was back in her place.

To conclude the dinner everybody, including the visitors, drank the health of Mademoiselle d'Angeville. It was ten o'clock, and since the guides might be dispersed elsewhere the next day, they decided to issue me with my accredited certificates of ascent before retiring for the night. They therefore declared on oath that they had taken me to the summit of Mont Blanc, and the mayor drew up a second document referring to this declaration and attesting that I was the first woman from outside the valley to complete this perilous exploit. All this was signed by the guides, the porters, and the council members: the signatures were duly attested, and the paper was stamped with the seal of the commune of Chamonix. A birth certificate or a marriage contract could not have been more authentic.

For their part, the guides and porters requested me to write my testimonial in their little books: you can imagine how willingly I furnished such well-deserved credentials! You have already made their acquaintance to some extent through the short biographies I provided earlier on; but it was only on my return that I was able to record the care, attention, and respect which they lavish on the visitors they accompany, the great willingness to please that they exhibit in every thing, and above all, the perfect propriety of voice and manner. During my ascent, when I spent three days and two nights, sometimes with eight, sometimes with one-and-twenty mountaineers, I neither *saw* nor *heard* anything that could not have been seen or heard in the most select salon company. This is a tribute that most visitors pay to the Chamonix guides and which I would particularly endorse where my own, whom I came to know so well on the slopes of Mont Blanc, were concerned. Nor must I forget an honourable mention of the two porters, whose strength and courage were so particularly valuable in the final struggle, given the general condition of the party as a whole.[5]

It was almost midnight when we took leave of each other, proud possessors of certificates of merit and valour. Once in my own room, I opened my Mont-Blanc notebook and continued with my notes, until my burning eyes found best solace in closing them and laying my head on the pillow.

Chapter XXVII

DIANE

Friday morning began for me with a visit to a third heroine of Mont Blanc, unsung by newspapers and public acclaim alike, to whom I am prompted by a spirit of justice to dedicate one short chapter in this account of our joint expedition.[1]

Here, then, is her portrait: two and a half years old, slender, active, bright-eyed and loose-limbed, with a pointed nose and red-brown coat. She answers to the name of Diane and had already distinguished herself in many a glorious chase after the hares of Chamonix, when M. Eisenkraemer, her master, took it into his head to take her up Mont Blanc with him.

Leaving Chamonix at the same time as he did, Diane had ranged over at least five-and-twenty miles by the time we reached the Pierre de l'Echelle, because, as is the wont of her kind, she ran around in front and behind, to cut off to right, to left, and diagonally, thus covering at least twice or thrice as much ground as we did.

On the Bossons glacier, she was supreme! She leapt crevasses with a rare agility, although not the widest of all, where she rode on the shoulders of one of the guides like a lost lamb found by the good shepherd. I forgot to find out how she fared on the difficult arête; and I did not catch up with her till the Grands Mulets where, you will doubtless remember, she partook of a good dinner and then disposed herself for sleep at her master's feet, where she stayed till it was time to move on.

With her natural exuberance somewhat dampened by the long walk of the previous day, Diane now eschewed useless detours, but forged ahead undaunted till she reached the Grand Plateau. I saw her again during the pause for breakfast, and she seemed to be suffering greatly: she turned round and round and whined, as though trying to lie down, but found the snow too cold, and gazed up at us with imploring eyes. From then on, she plodded after her master, step by step, tail and ears drooping. She scaled the ice wall unaided, and collapsed on the summit, totally worn out by fatigue; nor would she accept any food at such a height.

On the way down, she followed the party more cheerfully, and on the Grand Plateau, she even seemed to regain some of her old energy, for after they had crossed, a puff of wind carried off M. Eisenkraemer's hat: Diane chased off in pursuit, and was just about to pounce on it when it vanished into a crevasse. Diane was left whining on the edge.

From then on, there was nothing out of the ordinary to report, for she went close at her master's heels like a good dog, all the way back to Chamonix, where, if you remember, they reappeared the same evening.

When they reached the hotel, she lay down, refusing food, and slept for fifteen hours on end; woke, but still would not eat or drink; slept again, and continued in this pattern of sleep alternating with periods of fasting for the days after the ascent. When I went to see her, I found her in a state of lethargy reminiscent of my own on the ice wall. I called to her: she opened two tired eyes just for a moment; I stroked her, but she seemed unaware of my caress. It was plain that the poor creature was at the end of her strength. I really feared she might succumb; but when I left, she seemed a little better, and a few days later I was happy to hear that our four-legged heroine had made a full recovery.

I had sworn to treat Diane to an elegant dinner when she was capable of doing it justice, and so as soon as I had news that she was herself again, I sent her a roast chicken and a bowl of milk, all delicately set out on fine china and a linen tablecloth. I was curious to know how she would respond to this unwonted luxury, and my expectations were fulfilled when I learnt that she sat gazing at this tempting spread for a long time without daring to touch it. Having been well whipped as a puppy for stealing simpler fare, she doubtless thought that she was being put to the test; she was determined to emerge with her reputation intact! In the end the chicken had to be cut up and fed to her piece by piece and then her nose had to be pushed into the milk, before she could be convinced that this tantalizing banquet was not one of Old Nick's cunning wiles, sent to try her.

There has been much discussion about the instincts of our animal friends. For my part, I am inclined to rate them more highly than is common, and firmly believe them to be capable of reasoned judgement and of secondary ideas and even arguments, above all where their training is concerned. Diane is an example that can be adduced in support of this view.

Returning from my visit to Diane, I found Marie Paradis waiting for me; she had come to bid me farewell and to urge me to break my journey at her house in le Bourgeat, in order to sample some 'good fresh butter'. Since I intended, if the weather were favourable, returning via the Buet (going up by Valorsine and descending to Servoz), I communicated my intent to her, explaining that it rendered any firm engagement impossible. She exclaimed in horror over my idea of recuperation from Mont Blanc, assured me that the clouds would not lift for another week at least, and was so insistent that I pay her a visit, that I promised to do so if I should find myself obliged to take the common or garden way home.

Since this day was, at any rate, to be the last I spent at Chamonix, I occupied it by adding to the information I had collected on my first visit. The sublime recollections that I carried away from this lovely valley imbued the area with a fascination that was by no means merely geographical. Now, it was no longer only the peaks and glaciers that I held enshrined in my memories, it was also the manners and customs of this interesting people, its administration, its industry, and all its resources. I accordingly visited the mayor, the curé, and various other local dignitaries, with the aim of acquiring such information. All were kind enough to put themselves at my disposal. I then inspected the hotels and exhibitions of curiosities, and returned to my room to commit my impressions to paper.

These activities occupied the whole day. As I penned my last note, all the occupants of the Union Hotel, save me, lay fast asleep in their beds.

Chapter XXVIII

DEPARTURE

At last, the sad day of departure arrived. I was up at first light, and saw that the summits were veiled in cloud, but fortunately I was not contemplating climbing so high! So I abandoned my plans for the Buet and resigned myself to taking the high road. I bundled up my Mont Blanc costume, sent out for a carriage, and before leaving was at home to several new visitors, from the valley and further afield. Then I made my farewells to my guides, which they received with a display of emotion which touched me greatly. I reiterated my thanks for the tender care they had lavished upon me during our three-day expedition, and above all for the affection which they all expressed for my person. Speaking from the depths of my heart, I assured them that I would never forget them and would return to see them in 1840. Never will promise given be more gladly kept, for it will be a true pleasure to renew acquaintance with those worthy custodians of Mont Blanc and to return to the bosom of Chamonix.

All was ready for departure. There was a great press of people in front of the Union Hotel, courtiers from my day of glory on the 5th of September. I stepped into my carriage and was whisked away at top speed, for the vehicle was light, the horses young, and the postillion nineteen years old. Some of my guides lived in hamlets not far removed from Chamonix, and their families were on the look-out for my arrival. On the way, I encountered Couttet's wife with a gift of flowers and a pair of earrings in Mont-Blanc onyx. Further on, there was Desplan's wife, surrounded by her seven children; then Jacques Simond's family, and it gave me much joy to shake the hands of all these good people. I reached le Bourgeat, and halted the carriage once more to fulfil my promise to Marie Paradis. She ran to meet me with an expression of delight that amply repaid my kindness. I found her little house in a state of perfect cleanliness; her kitchen, like most of those in the valley, has no window, but only a great chimney with a shutter on a pulley to let the smoke out and admit air and light. A communicating door leads to a bedroom furnished with a stove, a clothes-press, and a large clock, and on either side of a little window, there stand two matching beds with, at the foot, two chests that serve as benches for a central table.[1] It was on this table that my dear Marie spread a red cloth, with a meal on it that I found much to my taste and very prettily laid out. I could not stay for long, for it was almost five o'clock when I left. With tears in her eyes, she embraced me, accompanied me to my carriage, and, wordlessly, embraced me once again!

'Goodbye, dear sister.' I said, genuinely affected by her emotion; 'In two years I shall return to take my place at your table once more!'

'Goodbye,' she replied, in a stifled voice.[2]

And we separated.

My young postillion carried me at such a pace, that I was soon out of my beloved valley. For the third time in six weeks I explored the delights of the road with a renewed pleasure, that was marred only by the troop of beggar-children who had pursued me on previous journeys and were once again on duty to spoil my enjoyment of the poetic beauty of the place.[3]

Oh parents, unworthy the name, educate your children to the dignity of work, rather than to the corruption of a profession degrading to all save the old or the sick, unable to provide for their needs by other means! Travellers, draw your purse-strings tight against these infant mendicants, for the coin that their importunity extracts from you will lead them into idleness, that most despicable of vices. But if one of them should offer you a pebble from the road that shines more brightly than its fellows, or a bunch of strawberries or flowers, do not reject him, for he is a budding entrepreneur. Encourage him from the start; purchase his paltry wares; pay threepence for what is worth a penny. Who knows? perhaps such good fortune will incline him for work and will save him both from idleness and the demeaning life of the mendicant.

At les Montées,[4] I found two children with trumpets who earn a little money for themselves by calling up the famous echo; I went through Servoz without stopping; at Chède, I saw the waterfall;[5] at Passy, the plum trees.[6] At last I reached Saint-Martin as night was falling, and took refuge in the Hotel Mont Blanc, where I found a large and cheerful company, an excellent supper, a clean room, a comfortable bed, and the best of landladies in the person of the Widow Trébilloud.

Chapter XXIX

RETURN TO GENEVA

The next day, the weather was superb, permitting a view from the hotel of the whole Mont Blanc range along the Montjoie valley. (Excepting the summits, which remained obstinately veiled in cloud.) I had been intending to take the diligence, but finding that there was a little barouche going in my direction, I profited by this discovery to take coach at a more congenial hour than the public stage, and in particular to stop wherever a delightful view seemed to invite a sojourn. Once again, the Nant d'Arpenaz was deemed worthy, and we trotted most leisurely through the charming Magland valley, where I gathered cyclamen in abundance. Between Cluses and Bonneville, I came across a whole army of young persons bearing flutes, clarionets, horns, and trumpets.[1] In the latter place, I stopped at the Hôtel de la Balance,[2] set out once more after two hours' rest, and fairly dashed the rest of the way home so as to reach Geneva a little earlier. At six o'clock, I was once more standing at the foot of my neighbour, the church-tower of Saint-Pierre, and, the same evening, I was in the arms of my dearest friends.

Here, then, I will end this account of my journey from Geneva to Mont Blanc, although it would take another volume to do justice to the display of interest occasioned by my return home. The welcome accorded to me by my friends was ample proof of their joy at having prophesied amiss. In society, I was visited and fêted, petted and spoiled, and I became aware that the general desire to know every last detail of my daring expedition was inspired as much by goodwill as by inquisitiveness. Wanting to preserve my recollections of it by means of brush and pencil, I had recourse to those numerous artists of distinction with which Geneva is blessed, and cannot but be gratified by the zeal with which they all approached a commission which was so flattering to their talents. This undertaking lasted three months, during which time my small triumph continued unabated. At last, however, I escaped to the lonely wastes of my beloved mountains, to savour once more the details of an expedition which bequeathed me the noblest and yet the sweetest memories in the world.

Henriette d'Angeville
Lompnès, March and April 1839

NOTES

INTRODUCTION

1. Mont Joli is 1368 toises (1 toise = 1949m) above sea-level. If the weather is favourable, there is a magnificent view from the summit. I went up it on the 30th of July and had the worst luck in the world: a thick mist which prevented any view, snow at one point, and eight hours on end of driving rain.
2. Le Jardin is an Alpine meadow, triangular in shape, which lies between the base of les Rouges and the upper part of the Talefre glacier. It is at an altitude of 1414 toises above sea-level. This excursion from Chamonix, including the return journey, takes thirteen hours' walking: five on a mule and the remaining eight on the *mer de glace* or through the snow. I made this trip on the 1st of August.
3. Lompnès, in the *département* of the Ain, which lies among fir-clad mountains between Nantua and Belley. Planachat, which is the highest point in the range, is 618 toises above sea-level, and the land at the Château de Lompnès, 450.
4. 'Tourists' is the name generally given to those travellers who make their way across a country for pleasure or instruction, and who, as the name suggests, follow a tour prescribed by guidebooks, itineraries, and maps. Switzerland, Savoy, and Italy abound in tourists.
5. Dr Hamel's scientific zeal induced him to attempt two ascents of Mont Blanc: the first from Saint-Gervais and the second from the Chamonix side. It was on the latter attempt that, towards the summit of the mountain, new-fallen snow, not as yet frozen firm with the old, slid downhill and carried all the climbers with it. Five of the unfortunate guides were swept into a crevasse, where three lost their lives; the Doctor, his two walking-companions, and the other guides were saved by a miracle.
6. On the 8th and 9th of October, 1834, the Count of Tilly ascended Mont Blanc without taking those precautions with regard to footwear

required by the simplest foray into the snow. As a result of this foolishness he returned with frost-bitten feet.
7. The name of my personal maid.

CHAPTER I

1. From Geneva itself (the higher part of the town), Mont Blanc cannot be seen; but from Rousseau's Island the summit and one of its shoulders are visible.
2. The Chamonix guides are organized into a proper society approved by the government, with a leader, a council, and regulations.

CHAPTER II

1. Between Cluses and Magland, you may see, at a height of about 700 feet in the mountain to the left of the road, the various openings of a famous grotto, often visited by travellers. In the vicinity there is an echo which may be demonstrated by the detonation of a cannon, shot from a certain angle, resulting in a prolonged rumbling. On my previous visit to Chamonix, I made my way up to this grotto and explored its whole extent.
2. For a moonlit journey of eighteen or twenty miles, over new-mended roads, they had the impudence to ask a price of fifty francs over and above the nineteen francs which was the official charge. Furthermore, they insisted that I should be responsible for any eventuality en route: that is, I should undertake to pay for the carriage and horses if a clumsy postillion should have them over.
3. Pray do not assume, from what I have just said, that the Savoyard inns are in general bad; on my two journeys, I found nothing but good care, good will, good beds, and moderate prices. The only exception was Master Lafin, and he must have regretted his behaviour towards me, for the trouble and expense occasioned by the journeys he made to the authorities in an attempt to clear his name did not save him from a stern rebuke, and involved him in costs which far exceeded the largest fine to which he was liable.

CHAPTER III

1. Of all the Chamonix guides, Couttet has made the largest number of ascents of Mont Blanc. The trip is thought to be so arduous and so perilous that few of them care to undertake it or to make a habit of it.
2. On my first visit to Chamonix, I had had much advice from Couttet on the ascent of Mont Blanc, and he had promised to lead my

party if ever I should decide to attempt it. I had not then fully made up my mind, and was in any case not contemplating an attempt until the following year.

CHAPTER IV

1. Having seen Julien Dévouassoud since I determined to write this account, I asked him if the inclusion of this public wager would distress him. 'Why should it? It's true, after all!', the good fellow replied, to his credit; and so I mention his response here. How many people, in all walks of life, lay claim to infallibility!

CHAPTER VI

1. See jacket illustration.
2. My birth certificate bears the date: 21 Ventôse, year 11 of the Republic, which corresponds to the 10th of March, 1794.
3. In the *Journal des Demoiselles*, the number for February 1839 (article entitled 'Maria of Mont Blanc').
4. *Le Propagateur* . . . This is perhaps not the only issue I might take up with this journal with reference to the article signed: *Exugua*, but I will refrain.

CHAPTER VII

1. Here are the names of the climbers Couttet had taken up Mont Blanc when I made my ascent: Count Matzewski, Mr Howard and Dr Rensselaer, Mr Undrell, Mr Clissold, Capt. Sherwill and Dr Clark, Messrs Fellows and Hawes, Mr Auldjo, Col. Wilbraham, and Dr Martin Barry.
2. With Mr Jackson.
3. It is interesting to observe that in many families where there are guides, the women-folk attend to the cultivation of the fields in the summer, and the men to household matters in the winter. In this reversal of roles, one counterbalances the other.
4. With Mr Auldjo.
5. With Capt. Sherwill and Dr Clark; Messrs Fellows and Hawes; and Messrs Hedrengen, Pidwel, and Atkins.
6. With Messrs Fellows and Hawes; Mr Auldjo; and Col. Wilbraham.
7. With Count Matzewski; Mr Howard and Dr Rensselaer; Mr Undrell; Mr Clissold; Dr Martin Barry; Count Henri of Tilly; and Mr Waddington.

CHAPTER VIII

1. The testimonials which Simond has received from the many travellers he has accompanied all agree on this point. Later (p. 85) it will become apparent that he feared neither fatigue nor even danger when he was concerned for the well-being of the people he was guiding.
2. Balmat (known as Balmat de Mont-Blanc), who recognized courage and energy when he saw it, was greatly attached to Mugnier, gave him his first lessons in mineralogy, and was wont to predict great things for him. I, too, feel that this excellent young man is destined to become the Balmat of the valley, not through new discoveries, but by virtue of the confidence and high esteem with which this Chamonix hero is rightly regarded by all.
3. When I questioned Mugnier about the age of the children in his care, he informed me that his little nephew was two-and-a-half years old. 'I trust,' I said, 'that when he is old enough to work, you will not lose him after having had all the trouble of his upbringing?' 'Oh, but when he is big enough to be useful to his parents, I expect to hand him back to them in exchange for a younger child, who would only be a burden to them otherwise.' I was overcome by this response, coming as it did from a simple mountain miller, for it bore witness to a more delicate sense of generosity than I could claim.

CHAPTER IX

1. I should warn my readers that this chapter contains nothing but details of no general interest, mostly concerned with the packing of provisions and with the clothes and equipment that I took up Mont Blanc. I have included these trivia for the benefit of those who are contemplating an ascent, or for those who like to know everything. Persons who are beginning to find that my activities at the Union hotel are becoming wearisome may spare themselves further tedium by turning without more ado to Chapter X.
2. I had been advised in Geneva to wear a pair of silk stockings under woollen ones, since they are less cumbersome and almost as warm as a second pair of woollen ones. After the event, I concur in this excellent advice, which I would recommend others to follow.
3. One, to be worn with a pair of silk stockings under woollen ones and gaiters tucked into the boots. The other, somewhat larger, would admit of an extra pair of stockings if need arose.
4. This veil was short, of double thickness, and had a drawstring round the lower edge to allow it to be fastened round my neck.

5. This hat was pretty much a parasol, that I turned round to follow the sun, without having the trouble of holding it.
6. M. Marin, owner of the baths bearing his name at Geneva, was kind enough to lend me his own, which is said by M. Noblet, the optician, to be one of the best in town. It magnifies twenty-eight times with perfect clarity.

CHAPTER X

1. At the start of the ascent, it is possible to go by mule as far as the Pierre Pointue. On the way back, one remounts much lower down.
2. Throughout my account, I use the Réamur thermometer. I shall therefore omit to specify it from now on. One degree Réamur × 1.25 = one degree Celsius.
3. In best possible health, and free from all anxieties, my pulse-rate is sixty a minute, remarkable for its slow steadiness. Sometimes it is only fifty-eight.
4. During my first sortie from Chamonix, I fetched up with an enormous mule that would have suited Goliath. I needed a ladder to clamber up on to the creature, whose heavy gait and bearing caused me much fatigue! These failings were compounded by frequent stumblings uphill, downhill, and on the flat, and you can imagine the torment that I suffered, since it is not permitted to argue the allocation of mules.

CHAPTER XI

1. Naturalists call these birds *lagopus*.
2. Except M. Eisenkraemer who was twenty-six or twenty-seven.
3. Moussa was taken back to the chalet at la Para, where her master collected her in the evening on his return from the Grands Mulets.
4. The main rock seemed to me to be about 25 feet high by 35 feet wide. Towards the bottom there is a little hollow, where they keep the ladder that is used to cross the Bossons glacier. It is for this reason that the rock is called the Pierre de l'Echelle.

CHAPTER XII

1. This last ascent has been made by M. Etienne Doulat, a Frenchman.

CHAPTER XIII

1. It is from the Count of Tilly that I have this height for the Grands Mulets, for I was not able to find it anywhere, and none of my guides could give me even an approximate idea.

2. I refer the reader to the song in which Madame Gibou tells how she makes the tea that she offers her guests.

CHAPTER XIV

1. A word from my private dictionary which expresses my meaning so perfectly that I shall look no further.
2. I have since discovered that the people of Chamonix call the Angelus the evening *arba* and the morning *arba* (according to the time of day). Being ignorant at the time of this dialect word, I was unable to make myself understood.
3. M. Atkins, who made the ascent the previous year (the 22nd and the 23rd of August, 1837) refers in his account to the 'Evening Hymn' which the guides sang at the Grands Mulets.
4. It is the very antiquity of this song which explains its content: it dates from the time when the people were taxed mercilessly.

CHAPTER XV

1. Mine was composed of a sheepskin spread on the rock in place of a bedstead, a blanket folded in four instead of a mattress and feather-bed, a second blanket to cover me, and one of the guides' bags at my head. What a luxurious bivouac for a lady! . . .
2. This first night at the Grands Mulets, I only heard three avalanches, and they all came from Mont Maudit: the first, during the singing, the second, which I mention here, and the third when we were on the point of departure.
3. M. Stoppen's tent would only accommodate two persons. M. Eisenkraemer had ordered none, and my own camp tents could only shelter four. Everyone else slept in the open, under the stars.

CHAPTER XVI

1. The formation of these bridges is a mystery which I leave others, wiser than me, to solve.
2. Séracs are blocks of ice of enormous size, and generally rectangular in shape.
3. M. Rey, the author of several respected works, was kind enough to let me see a chapter of his history of the hospice at the Great Saint Bernard, in which he refutes, successfully, as it seems to me, the opinion of the guides that it is dangerous to provoke the breaking of an avalanche by the slightest disturbance of the air. If it were really so, he says, one single rumble of thunder in the middle of the Alps would

release all the snow lying at the top of slopes. He reminds us that huge armies passed through the Alps, at all periods and in all directions, and that the cannon roared in every valley, without a single accident having been recorded as a result. What, he asks, is the sound of a bell or of the human voice, compared to the rending of a crumbling glacier, the crash of a thunderbolt, or the cannon's mighty voice? He concludes that such an opinion should be relegated to those misconceptions deplored by common sense and experience alike.

CHAPTER XVII

1. The Corridor is the narrow passage between Mont Maudit and the ice wall.
2. Les Rognes are outcrops on the upper part of the arête joining the summit of Mont Blanc to the Dôme du Gôuter. There are two principal ones, the others being hardly more than undulations.

CHAPTER XIX

1. A few moments before, I had crossed with M. Eisenkraemer who was sliding down. M. Stoppen also left the summit as I arrived, so that I was alone on it with the six guides and two porters who composed my little troupe.

CHAPTER XX

1. You will remember that the white sheet spread out in the meadow by the church was the agreed signal for the pigeon's return to the dovecote.
2. For the reader who is curious to know the fate of the bird, I can say that it was first sighted in the little village of les Bossons; two days later at les Praz-d'en-bas; then the following week at les Ouches, where they tried to catch it. But the attempt frightened it, and it flew off, to be seen no more in the valley.

A few weeks later, it was learnt that a wild pigeon had been killed on the roof of the curé's house in les Contamines, and eaten by the local pastor. Enquiries as to its plumage revealed that it was identical with the one we had lost. Mention was also made of a thread on its foot, which removed all cause for doubt. To end up in the pot eight weeks after the ascent: such was the sad fate of our poor feathered friend!

I subseqeuntly learnt that instead of a steady old bird as I had requested, I had been given a yearling. It was its very youth that caused its loss.

3. The Jura is much lower than several other mountains visible in the same direction. It is by the ordinary optical effect of falling perspective that its outlines seem to dominate the view.
4. Not as deep here, however, as I saw it at le Jardin on the 3rd of August that same year. This difference may be accounted for by the enclosed situation of the latter.
5. It is claimed that sounds are not as loud at the height of Mont Blanc. I cannot tell how it may be for sharp sounds, like a firearm or a trumpet; but I can say that I noticed no difference where the human voice was concerned; and that, both close to and at a distance, I could always hear my guides perfectly.
6. It should be observed that, with the exception of Couttet, who is unusually well-adapted for Mont Blanc, the disorders experienced by the rest of my party were in direct proportion to their age. The porters only felt a minor sleepiness which they overcame without difficulty. Desplan, who was not yet forty, had cramps and mild discomforts which afterwards vanished; but the others suffered more severely, above all Tronchet, the eldest. For an instant I was afraid that he was undergoing an apoplectic fit, when I saw him in the state I have just described.
7. I can say this without boasting, for I see no merit in a reasonably sound physique; merit lies rather in overcoming a weak one.

CHAPTER XXI

1. When about to climb the wall, the guides, suffering as they were, left behind their bags, and even my pelisse, which I missed much on the summit.
2. Les Miquelets: a band of mountain partisans in the Roussillon.

CHAPTER XXII

1. The bottle of alcohol ran out before the water was even warm.
2. Apart from the poalaxa and the *Saxifraga bryoïdes*, from the Grands Mulets, I also found the following flowers: *Potentilla grandiflora, Myosotis alpestris, Phyteuma hemisphericum, Hutchinsia alpina, Gentiana campestris, Polygonum viviparum, Achillea moscata, Sempervivum montanum, Campanula linifolia, Cirastium latifolium, Rhododendron ferrugineum, Geum montanum, Pyrethrum alpinum, Erica vulgaris, Pinguicula vulgaris, Pedicularis rostratum, Ranunculus glacialis, Linaria alpina, Saxifraga stellaris*. I owe these identifications to Professor de Candolle.

CHAPTER XXIII

1. I have preserved a branch of Erica from the bouquet so graciously offered by Lady C*** in my Mont-Blanc herbal.
2. On my descent from Mont Blanc, the only sentiment I inspired in the good folk of Chamonix was one of curiosity. Since then, I have, I hope, left happy memories and, perhaps, some affection.

CHAPTER XXIV

1. It continued more strongly into the evening, and unabated all night. The next day it fell in torrents! The day after, there was a terrible wind, and for two weeks one could not see the summit, but only, through the glass, the marks of a huge avalanche, which had come down an estimated five hundred feet from the dome of Mont Blanc, swept across the Grand Plateau, and hurtled down above the Grands Mulets, thus wiping out our whole path! It must be agreed that Providence really smiled on my expedition to Mont Blanc!
2. The fidelity of her account was afterwards confirmed by several other persons.
3. Jeannette had the delicacy to conceal from me the fact that she, pious creature, was the first to suggest that masses should be said for the success of the trip. I found this out later, from witnesses who were at the priest's house when she arrived with this touching demonstration of devotion to her mistress. I am glad to record it here as a tribute to her good character and warm heart.
4. It is from the top of the ice wall that those on the mountain and in Chamonix can once again see each other.
5. I explained the delay to our ascent in my account. M. Eisenkraemer made the path, cutting a hundred and fifty steps himself. M. Stoppen halted out of precaution and I did so out of necessity.
6. The ascent of the 4th of September 1838, is the largest ever made. It had been known for several travellers to join forces and take seven, eight, or nine guides for all of them! but never three distinct parties reaching the summit on the same day.
7. For two days I suffered from blurred vision, and saw things double. I also saw blue, yellow, red, green and black spots before my eyes. This strange condition made writing extremely difficult.

CHAPTER XXV

1. This woman has wrongly been referred to as Marie Couttet in several guides or handbooks which mention her ascent.

2. I have transcribed this conversation in all its simplicity, without improving the language or romanticizing the person of this dear old lady.
3. Certain details about herself, given to me by Marie Paradis and omitted here because they are not relevant to my purpose, confirm her complete honesty. I have great confidence in her account which was, incidentally, borne out by one of the guides who went up Mont Blanc with her.
4. In making this comparison, Marie demonstrated a heavy, much impeded respiration.

CHAPTER XXVI

1. Although David Couttet was not one of my party, I invited him because he contributed very greatly to the success of our three ascents. You will recall that it was he and Jean Mugnier who went ahead to lay a track from the Grands Mulets to the Petit Plateau.
2. When you think of the risks incurred by these noble guides in order to satisfy the phantasy of an ascent, and recall the devotion with which they perform this dangerous and difficult duty, one would fain have all the riches of Golconda to lavish on them. For my part, I do not feel money is a sufficient recompense, and shall always hold them in the tenderest and most grateful regard.
3. *Lagna*: word in the Chamonix patois meaning *tired, out of breath.*
4. *Sonzon*: another such word, meaning *summit.*
5. In view of what I said of Jean Mugnier at the outset (Chapter VIII), and the many services he performed during the ascent, you will understand the pleasure I had in obtaining his admission into the first class of guides. I requested this from the Governor of Savoy, with an account of the just reasons for his elevation. His Excellency granted it in a manner most flattering to my protégé, by informing him that he had earned this promotion by reason of his *personal merits.*

CHAPTER XXVII

1. Those who are interested in the natural sciences may be curious to know the effect of an ascent to 15,000 feet on a member of the canine race. Hence this chapter on Diane.

CHAPTER XXVIII

1. These internal arrangements, and the furnishings which I describe here, are almost the same throughout the Chamonix valley.

2. This farewell was to be the last. I was never to see poor Marie again. Since I penned these lines, letters from Chamonix informed me that on the 25th of March, 1839, she succumbed to a dropsy of the chest. Two weeks before her death, one of the guides went to see her, and said that he intended writing to me. She asked him to wait for the outcome of her illness, so as to be able to let me know the best or the worst (her own expression, poor Marie!). I am glad that I gave her one of the last pleasures she had on earth, and also that I had the foresight to have her likeness taken.

3. In the Chamonix valley, the children have a little shop selling all the flowers, fruit, or crystals you could want. On the remainder of the road, they are importunate little beggars, who run after you asking for alms or sweetmeats. I have seen as many as eleven at a time, hands outstretched around my carriage; they included girls of sixteen to eighteen, and several fifteen-year-old boys.

4. Between les Ouches and Pont Pelissier, there is an echo which sounds prettily to a trumpet-call. Two children are always on the look-out for travellers here.

5. To take me to the waterfall at Chède, I chose a little lad of ten, whose amusing chatter entertained me much as we went. When we separated, I said: 'Well, my little guide, what do you want for your pains?'

'Whatever you want, Madame.'

'No, you must set the rate.'

'Lord! It's up to your generosity.'

'Well then, tell me what would make you really pleased, really happy. I am in luck at the moment, you shall have what you want.' He scratched his ear, then looked up:

'Well!', he said, greatly daring, 'give me *thruppence*!' (and then he stopped as if alarmed by his boldness, and looked up to see how I might react).

'Threepence! Is that all you want, my child? Here, take a shilling, you will be happier still.'

The little fellow blushed crimson, took the coin, and shot off, forgetting his thanks in his transports of delight at such good fortune! I felt happy to have caused him so much pleasure for so little expense, and to have kept faith with my given word.

I will spare the reader the thoughts on relative ambition which ensued.

6. Almost all the area round Passy is covered with profitable plum

trees. I am assured that the sale of plums from the village brings in an income of 6,000 francs in an average year.

CHAPTER XXIX

1. I learnt at Bonneville that these young musicians were intending to give me a concert as I passed through the town, or else at Chamonix where they were going for two days.
2. I can recommend gastronomes to try the delicious semolina soup prepared in this hotel.